SECRETS FOR CAT SITTING SUCCESS

SECRETS FOR CAT SITTING SUCCESS

Your Business Guide
for Profit & Purrs

Diane O'Callahan, M.Ed.

Owner of Pets & Petals, North Hampton, NH

ISBN 979-8-9990829-0-9
Library of Congress Control Number 2025912131
Printed in United States of America

Editorial services by Renee M. Nicholls (www.mywritingcoach.net)
Book design by C'est Beau Designs (www.cestbeaudesigns.com)

Published by Pets & Petals (petspetals@gmail.com)
Visit www.petsandpetals.us

To all the wonderful families
who have given me the privilege of caring for their cats,
fish, cows, seahorses, and plants over the years.

CONTENTS

PREFACE

As you read this book, you will learn essential skills and secrets in providing pet care that will exceed your customers' expectations and differentiate yourself from your competitors. Using tips from this book, you will pay attention to cat care as well as plant and house details that will transform your clients into loyal fans. By following the initial steps to set up your business, you will enhance your skills in communication and make essential contacts. Your time and money management skills will grow as you learn to juggle pet sitting with your other daily responsibilities.

In the pages that follow, you will read engaging stories about the fun times you can have with the kitties, and you will learn specific ways to enrich and entertain their lives as well as yours. You will become alert to emergency situations with the kitties and their homes, which will prepare you for what to do in the face of similar scenarios and help you prevent such calamities. You will develop skills in trust building and integrity by being reliable and flexible, keeping your word, and handling unexpected situations in a professional way.

For me, being the business owner of a cat and plant care service that I created from the beginning is thrilling and rewarding. As you will discover here, it takes a combination of courage, commitment, and ongoing dedication to the needs of the cats and clients to sustain a successful business venture. When I started my cat sitting and plant care business, Pets & Petals, in the early 1990s, there was only one other pet sitter in my area. I had to develop this business by being creative and using a trial-and-error method. I learned from each new experience and developed ways to navigate in uncharted territories.

Several years later, I attended the Professional Pet Sitters International (PSI) Conference, and the information they shared reassured me that I was on the right track. In my quest to learn even more about animal care, I became a volunteer to take care of cats at the New Hampshire Society for the Prevention of Cruelty to Animals (New Hampshire SPCA). Soon afterward, I applied to be the first full-time Humane Education Coordinator hired at the New Hampshire SPCA to teach elementary children about pet care through K.I.N.D Clubs. I created Jr. Volunteer Programs for middle and high school students to learn about and care for the animals at the shelter.

In this position, I was able to interact with and learn more about cats and other animals, such as degus, hamsters, guinea pigs, birds, rabbits, ferrets, rats, mice, chinchillas, dogs, hedgehogs, and fish, on a regular basis!

Today, it is my great pleasure to be able to share my wealth of experience and secrets for a successful business with you. Since the days in the 1990s when I first launched my business, I have always been grateful for the opportunity to work as a professional cat sitter. I find joy in being greeted at the door by happy, curious kitties, and in creating and participating in kitty playtimes that bring meows and purrs all around. Throughout this book, I will not only teach you how to set up your own fun and profitable pet sitting business but also share some of my unexpected adventures taking care of indoor plants, seahorses, and even cows!

Secrets for Cat Sitting Success: Your Business Guide for Profit & Purrs opens with a series of questions to help you determine if running a cat sitting business is the right fit for you. Then, in the chapters that follow, I will teach you how to start out, from setting yourself up with the necessary forms to advertising, obtaining supplies, and figuring out the ins and outs of how best to run your business. From the very first Meet & Greet to a full day in the life of a professional cat sitter, I will describe some of the adventures I have experienced with my feline clients, the families' plants, and sometimes even their houses. This guide shares thirty years of escapades and challenges, and it provides valuable knowledge to assist you in creating the cat sitting and plant care service of your dreams.

The stories I share are often humorous, with amusing and occasionally startling accounts of actual events. As you read about my own joys, challenges, and dilemmas, I hope these experiences will help you develop a successful business model, avoid similar mistakes, and protect your brand. Along the way, I will also include information to help you find important resources, such as insurance policies, online forums, contracts, daily pet care journal forms, tax considerations, advertising opportunities, business networks, and emergency plans.

This book will get you ready to create a cat sitting service that is both fun and profitable. Are you ready for an "un-fur-gettable" career as a professional pet sitter? Let's dive right in and find out.

INTRODUCTION:

IS PET SITTING FOR YOU?

Pet sitting may be an ideal fit for you if you can answer yes to the following questions.

1. **Do you have time?** You will need several hours open to work at the beginning and the end of the day. Expect to spend at least 30 to 60 minutes per visit (plus driving time) to feed the kitties, to scoop the litter, and to play and visit with each kitty.

2. **Are your hours reliable?** You will need to be able to maintain an organized, reliable (and yet somewhat flexible) schedule.

3. **Do you have reliable transportation?** This is a must-have. Ideally, you will also have a plan for backup transportation.

4. **Are startup funds available?** You will need money or credit at hand for your startup. These costs, which will be covered in more detail in later chapters, do not all have to be accrued by Day 1, but you should definitely plan to have

funds available to you throughout the year for expenses like the following:

- Joining a professional pet sitters' organization
- Enrolling in a pet first aid course
- Getting a business name and setting up an LLC (a Limited Liability Company: a business structure to protect and separate your business assets from your personal assets)
- Designing a website with hosting, SSL, and malware protection
- Paying an accountant or a bookkeeper
- Obtaining pet sitter liability insurance
- Paying for a background check
- Creating or purchasing a pet sitting service contract
- Paying internet and cellphone fees
- Advertising
- Maintaining a car and buying gas
- Buying additional supplies for cat care
- Buying clients gifts for holidays and as incentives for referrals

A sample budgeting chart with these expenses appears in Appendix A. You can probably plan on spending approximately $8,000 over the first year; depending on your goals and the size and scope of your business plan, the fees may climb even higher. The good news is that if you are resourceful, you can pare back some of these expenses by taking on some of the tasks you would need to otherwise pay a professional to do, such as creating a do-it-yourself website, adapting a standard contract, printing your own business cards and flyers, and filing your own taxes, and by waiting a year or two before you start giving holiday gifts to your clients. Further, your business-related expenses, including space for a home office, will likely be tax deductible.

5. **Are you prepared to keep detailed financial records?** In the beginning, you may find it worthwhile to speak with a tax professional, bookkeeper, or accountant to determine what expenses you need to keep track of and how any expenses, taxes, and deductions may affect your budgeting plans. Then you will need to keep track of your finances and expenditures and/or use a bookkeeper or an accountant for tax purposes.

6. **Are you knowledgeable about cat care and plant care (or willing to learn)?** Clients will expect you to come to the job with a professional level of expertise. You should also plan to take a pet first aid course through your local rescue groups, online through Pet Sitters International, or in a Red Cross class. Later in the book, I will also discuss certification programs. Further, you may wish to offer indoor plant care services to your pet sitting clients at no additional fee. I enjoy watering houseplants, and I always appreciate their beauty. However, if watering geraniums, orchids, Christmas cactuses, palm plants, and other indoor and outdoor plants at people's homes will be new territory for you, then you also may need to study up on these plants to make sure they are still healthy when their owners return.

7. **Are you comfortable communicating with clients, veterinarians, and other referral sources?** As you will discover in the pages that follow, effective communication will be a key to your professional success.

8. **Are you prepared to work evenings, weekends, and holidays?** Due to a surge in pet sitting requests during these periods, you will likely miss certain holidays and social and family events, so you will need to be flexible about scheduling your own celebrations for different times.

How did you do? If you have answered "Yes" to these questions or have solid plans to address them, then it may be the "purr-fect" time for you to create your own business. In the chapters that follow, I'll show you how.

CHAPTER ONE

STARTING YOUR BUSINESS

I was very excited to receive my first pet sitting calls. Over the phone, I confirmed that the potential clients' kitties were indoor only, that the cats did not have serious medical concerns, and that the family was in my service area of a ten-mile radius. Then I prepared for a Meet & Greet by getting organized: I located my Pets & Petals flyer, business card, Pet Sitting Information Form, and Veterinarian Release Form, as well as a secure baggie to store their key. I arrived at their home at the agreed-upon time. As I was greeted, I introduced myself and handed the client my card. Once inside the house, I presented my flyer and took careful notes to be sure I remembered the kitty-care instructions. I requested and received all the answers I needed to complete my Pet Sitting Information Form, and I had them complete and sign my Veterinarian Release Form.

In those early days, I was very happy to meet new clients and their kitties. I was anxious to see if the cats and I could become friends and playmates while their pet parents were vacationing—and I was both relieved and excited when we did. As I continued to build up Pets & Petals through referrals from my veterinarian and word of mouth from my satisfied clients, it was a phenomenal time of learning, love, and high energy as visits increased. Before too long, some days found me taking care of and playing with sweet kitties for up to ten hours!

Hopefully, this all sounds as wonderful to you as it does to me. With that in mind, to ensure financial success, I recommend that if you already have a full-time job, you first build up a solid basis of cat sitting clients by treating it as a side gig. Then, once you have built up a sufficient, dependable clientele, you can seriously consider leaving your current job so you can focus on your pet sitting business full-time. The good news is that the first step I'll advise in this chapter, creating a business plan, can "pawsitively" help you reach that crucial point even sooner.

CREATING A BUSINESS PLAN

A business plan is a formal, written document that lists your business goals, the approach you will take to achieve them, and your proposed time frame. Having a business plan is valuable for cat sitters since it helps you stay focused on your goals and outcomes.

If you'd like to see online examples of professional small-business plans, sample cases are currently available through the U.S. Small Business Association's website at www.sba.gov/business-guide/plan-your-business/write-your-business-plan. As you create a business plan for your cat sitting business, you will want to include the following:

- **Your area of service, within a selected-mile radius of your home.** To make this determination, consider potential weather conditions, anticipated pet medical needs, and the time required for the care of each animal. Then make calculations to confirm that the travel distance would be worth your time and commitment. Specifically, you should verify the distance to a neighborhood at the edge of your proposed area to be sure that the actual cost per mile would be economical for your budget and travel time. For example, if fuel costs $3.89 per gallon and you drive 20 miles round trip for one pet sit, the cost per mile would be about $3.11 (source: Fuelcostcalculator.org). Currently, the IRS lets you deduct $.70 per mile traveled in 2025. However, your actual cost is likely $1.00 a mile (or more) when you consider all costs, including insurance, depreciation, maintenance, and fuel. Be sure to set a location boundary that allows you to charge a fee that not only permits you to make money but also is in line with other pet sitters' fees in your area.

- **Your scope of services.** What pets would you like to take care of? Will your services include collecting the mail, watering the indoor and outdoor plants, and taking out the recycle and trash bins? What about other unique tasks, such as feeding their wild birds? Will you offer overnight stays? Are you willing to job share if they want to have a neighbor or relative stop by to take on one of the care shifts? I always make it clear that I need to be the only provider. My insurance does not cover me when other people are sharing my job, because the insurance company cannot determine who is at fault if a problem arises with the cat or with the house. At times, I also agree to water outdoor plants while clients are away. If you believe the outdoor watering tasks are likely to take you more than ten minutes, then you may want to make arrangements with the client to charge an extra fee.

- **Your annual budget.** To make this determination, include your anticipated cost of supplies, tax preparation, vehicle use, and fee schedule. More details on the expenses you can expect as a cat sitter appear in the chapters that follow, and a sample budget with estimated expenses appears at the end of this book. For your business to be profitable, you will need your expected income to exceed your expected expenditures, including any taxes.

- **An assessment of your competition.** It's important to know what services other cat sitters are offering to clients so you can adjust your business accordingly. Research what openings exist in your area, what a competitive fee would be, and how you can advertise your new business.

- **Legal concerns**. According to uspto.gov, "Using a business name doesn't necessarily qualify as trademark use but using it as the source of goods or services might qualify it as both a business name and a trademark." If you are concerned about trademarking your business name, then it would be wise to explore your state's business website or the federal website (www.uspto.gov) to purchase a trademark for your business name. I have a trademark for my business name, Pets & Petals, through my state. You should also check your state to see if your company needs to be registered.

I appreciated my local Small Business Administration, SCORE (a group of retired businesspeople who offer assistance for free), as I was writing a business plan and had other legal concerns. You can find ways to reach them at www.sba.gov/business-guide.

SECURING RESOURCES AND TRANSPORTATION

Before you dive in, you will also want to take steps to ensure you have sufficient financial resources to keep your business afloat. It is important not to leave your clients (or yourself!) in the lurch because you haven't put enough time and money aside for unexpected challenges like car repairs. Along those lines, unless you are limiting your service area to a route that is walkable or accessible by public transportation, you will need a car that is in good condition. You may also need an Uber or Lyft account or friends and family members who can lend you their car if your car breaks down or during a weather emergency with downed trees across your driveway.

INCREASING YOUR KNOWLEDGE

It's always best to educate yourself as much as possible on any issues you feel you may encounter with a kitty, plant, or house. As noted, I firmly believe all pet sitters should take a pet first aid class before they start work in this field. Whenever I am faced with a new challenge, I always think about the issue from the pet's point of view first, and then my client's point of view. I also try to think ahead to avert future problems.

As part of my daily work, I research as much as I can to be sure the pets and plants have excellent care. I also consult with professionals, such as the clients' veterinarians (or my own), plant nurseries, and people knowledgeable about houses. I enjoy learning more about feline medical, emotional, and behavioral issues, by studying books, taking online seminars, and reading professional pet sitting magazines (see the Resources section). I make sure I am a good student during visits to my veterinarian, and I have also learned a great deal from the wonderful coworkers I met through the New Hampshire SPCA.

As part of my ongoing commitment to staying informed, I subscribe to the monthly magazine of Pet Sitter International (PSI), and I have attended the PSI conferences to get familiar with current pet sitting trends. In *Pet Sitter's World* magazine, there is always a section on insurance liability claims, which is very informative. It gives tips on trouble other pet sitters have encountered so that I can avoid these mistakes. In fact, each issue is chock full of "paw-some" articles. For example, the articles I am reading right now involve working with clients, animal behavioral concerns, pet safety, free member resources and webinars, marketing and social media posts, scams to avoid, and emergency backup plans.

At this publication date, there are no official state requirements to become a pet sitter. However, I strongly encourage cat sitters to continue their education so that when animal concerns arise, you are confident and prepared to offer the best care possible.

Pet Sitters International (PSI) and National Association of Professional Pet Sitters (NAPPS) are organizations that have certification programs with courses and an exam covering topics such as pet care, health, nutrition, and behavior for a variety of animals. Some pet sitters decide to pursue this option. This certificate can be advertised on your business card, flyer, and website and may allow you to receive a discount on your insurance policy.

Because I also offer plant care services, I have learned how to keep exotic plants alive by purchasing them and learning their needs for humidity, watering, sunlight, and placement indoors. As I care for people's property, I research each problem as it crops up, and I also consider how I would want my own property treated. You will find stories about some of these situations later in the book.

Consider your investment in further education as an investment in yourself and your business. Your continued education through pet and plant care seminars, books, online reading, and memberships in local pet sitters' groups and either NAPPS or PSI will help you in conversations with new clients—and ultimately assist your business in growing even more.

OBTAINING INSURANCE AND BONDING

To protect myself financially, each year I purchase a Liability Protection Policy for the Pet Service Professional as a Sole Proprietor. This includes coverage for pets and property in my care, custody, or control. It also includes payouts for limited veterinary medical coverage. I firmly believe this insurance is a must for the safety of the animals in your care and the security of your clients. If you join Pet Sitters International (www.petsit.com), there is an option to purchase pet sitters' insurance as an individual pet sitter through several different companies. Medical insurance is also offered.

The PSI newsletter, along with their forum about pet care, often includes cautionary tales about cat care visits that have gone awry. A few examples of the cost of the damage include "a pet sitter giving the kitty too much insulin medication – Paid $13,433; a pet sitter leaving the toilet running, which caused water damage to the contents of the client's house – Paid $29,832." Other tales with expensive outcomes include cats that escaped and later required veterinary care, frozen pipes that burst when they were left unattended, and a job-sharing situation where the substitute cat sitter left the freezer door open, which defrosted all the frozen food.

Without insurance, mistakes like these can cost the cat sitter money as well as jeopardizing their brand and reputation. Although pet sitters' business insurance does not cover every situation, I find that since I am the first line of defense in the pet's safety and the client's home and plant care, the insurance does offer peace of mind for both me and my client. Having insurance will also add a professional feature to your business. Be sure to advertise that you have these protections on your business cards, flyers, and website, and be ready to present a copy of your policy when asked.

Some states also require bonding. Bonding is a guarantee to your clients that if you, an employee, or an independent contractor steal from them, then they would be paid for the stolen item if you have a high enough bond limit. (The terms and payouts may vary depending on the bond.) For pet sitters starting out, getting bonded is a great selling point to promote your professionalism and honesty to new clients.

PLANNING FOR TIME MANAGEMENT CHALLENGES

The business of working with cats and plants in people's homes is wonderful, but it requires a true commitment to their scheduling needs. Each new client is an opportunity to practice your pet and plant care skills and provide excellent services so that they will rehire you and refer you to other clients.

As I've noted, vacation weeks and dependable days of time off are something you may not be able to count on when you are building your business. Your advertising efforts to recruit clients and referral sources might be in vain if you don't provide excellent cat and plant care services on weekends, holidays, and periods when most people are taking time off.

I highly suggest that you team up with a qualified, trustworthy backup person you can rely on to step in for you as needed, plus another pet sitter to whom you can refer clients if you get overbooked or need time off for any reason. My husband, Christopher, has been my reliable backup person, along with my friend and neighbor, Anita Hubbard. Anita has even volunteered to cover my clients—with the client's knowledge and permission—when I have had a family funeral to attend. I cannot thank Anita enough. After an introduction to the kitties and their homes—providing training on the alarm systems as needed—I knew the kitties would be well cared for by Anita. I also suggest to my clients that they each identify a friend, relative, or another pet sitter as a backup for me so that they will always have coverage.

Time management challenges can get easier as your business becomes established. I always let my clients know well ahead when I am taking vacation time. This communication allows them to plan their getaways around those dates or, if they prefer, to get someone else to cover. In the beginning, I put my vacation or out-of-office message on my voicemail greeting when I was away, but then I realized this isn't secure for my home office. Now, I communicate my time-off schedule with everyone personally.

POLISHING YOUR COMMUNICATION SKILLS

To make the best impression with clients, it's important to communicate clearly, frequently, and professionally. Here are ten great tips you can follow.

1. Always be friendly, polite, and enthusiastic—focusing on the people as well as the kitties.

2. Turn off or silence your phone to give them your full attention.

3. Make eye contact throughout the conversation.

4. Listen carefully, taking notes so you don't forget anything.

5. Request clarification if something confuses you. Ask, "Have I understood this correctly?" and "Is there anything else you feel I should know?"

6. Remain upbeat and speak positively.

7. In both your body language and your tone, exude confidence—and calmness.

8. Keep conversations focused on the cats as much as possible.

9. Avoid gossip and offensive language.

10. Make sure the cat care journal forms you share are always legible. If you are using a computer to communicate, always run the spell-check.

This simple but effective advice—combined with the other skills included throughout the book—will help you make sure you always put your best foot forward. When you build a reputation as someone who always acts and communicates in a professional manner, the clients are much more likely to refer you to their friends and family—and, most important, to hire you again.

CHAPTER TWO

SETTING UP YOUR BUSINESS

Once you have established a business plan, financial resources, reliable transportation, knowledge of animal and plant care, time management tools, and communication skills, the fun and creative process to start your "purrfessional" career can begin.

CHOOSING A BUSINESS NAME

My mother, Lee Dougherty, suggested a name that represented my services: Pets & Petals. I checked out this name online to confirm that, at least in my area, my choice was original; this helped to ensure that it would be well received by search engines and potential clients. Some online platforms (e.g., Wix) now offer business name generators that use AI, so you can check those out if you feel you need more help.

TRADEMARKING YOUR BUSINESS NAME WITH YOUR STATE

Common rights to a trademark begin as soon as a business starts to use the mark in advertising, so you are not required to register your brand or logo. However, registration offers you rights and protections, such as filing an action in state court for infringement and damages against another party. The office of your Secretary of State offers the state trademark registration application online. I found this process easy, and currently it is renewable in my state every five years for $50.00.

CREATING A BUSINESS LOGO AND SELECTING BRAND COLORS

I learned that black-and-white creations cost less for printing, but colors highlight your design. To save costs, you may want to check out online platforms like Design.com and Canva, which use AI to quickly generate hundreds of options. Locally, I enjoy working with Elite Printing LLC. They helped me design my logo for car magnets, business cards, and a banner (also see the next section). With this company, the logo design is mine to keep and to use on any advertising with no extra permission or fees required, so be sure to ask your designer if this is the case for your design. Once you've narrowed down your choices, you may want to poll friends, family, and potential clients to ask which ones they prefer, and why.

DESIGNING BUSINESS CARDS AND FLYERS

In this step, I was able to be very creative. There are lots of options and ideas from online services such as VistaPrint.com; you might also wish to contact a local printer. Here's a sample of my business card:

As you can see, it lists my services, notes that I am insured, states that I have references from veterinarians, and has space for my phone numbers, email address, and website. I have veterinary references because the staff at my cats' animal hospital, who are now very familiar with my work, agreed to place me on their list of recommended pet sitters. Then, as they received more and more positive feedback about my services from their clients, they moved me to the top of the list. They also allowed me to put my business cards into the holders at their office (which has been a great marketing tool). You could ask to be put on the list of several animal hospitals in your area—and keep their business card holders filled, too!

My very creative brother, designed my flyer, which I still use today—so you may even be lucky enough to rely on artistic friends or family members. My brother captured the cat sitting and plant care features of my business very effectively, with a written description of exactly what my clients may expect from my services.

Pets ♥ Petals

Affordable Animal and Plant Care in Your Home

Convenient & Reliable

If you're like most animal lovers, you hate having to leave your pet in new or unfamiliar surroundings when you travel. **Pets & Petals** provides your cat(s), other small mammals, or plants, the care they need while you're away, right in your own home. I truly love animals and am a pet parent to several cats.

With **Pets & Petals**, you receive reliable, responsible service and peace of mind. With us, your pets

- *stay in a secure, familiar environment,*
- *follow their usual routine and diet,*
- *avoid exposure to kennel illnesses, and*
- *receive loving, individual attention and playtimes with cat enrichment games*

How Pets & Petals Works

When you call **Pets & Petals**, I will arrange a visit to your home shortly before you leave, to

- *meet you and your pet(s),*
- *obtain detailed information about caring for your pet(s) and plants, and*
- *agree on the care schedule and fee*

While you're away, **Pets & Petals** will

- *feed and water your pet(s) and plants,*
- *exercise and play with your pet(s),*
- *give medicines, vitamins, or other special care, and obtain veterinarian care in case of illness.*

Home Security

While I am visiting, I am happy to make your home look "lived-in" by getting the mail, putting out barrels and adjusting draperies and lights.

To Arrange for Service...

Please call **Pets & Petals** as soon as you plan your trip to reserve pet care dates. Call us today at

Cell Phone:
555-555-1212

MEMBER- PET SITTERS INTERNATIONAL-- INSURED

At a minimum, you will want to start out with business cards and flyers. In the next chapter, I will also share what other marketing tools I tried, and which ones worked best for me.

CREATING THE NECESSARY FORMS

To ensure that your transactions are professional and binding, you'll need documents such as information forms, release forms, contracts, journal forms, and invoices. In this section I will show you some samples.

Pet Sitting Information Form

Before I meet with a client, I create a Pet Sitting Information Form, which outlines the client's information and the pet's daily care schedule, along with any other duties I will be performing while I am at their home. (See Appendix B.) I fill in as many details as I have available, and then I complete the rest of the form at the Meet & Greet.

CAT SITTING CONTRACT

A contract is an agreement between you and the client so there are no misunderstandings. If you ever find yourself in a legal dispute, you will have written documentation on hand to resolve it more easily. Since the contract is unique to the services you provide, there are a few options for you to consider: You can review the online templates that are available through Pet Sitters International (www.petsit.com) and then purchase a contract from them, you can design a contract yourself, or you can consult an attorney. I have included a sample contract in Appendix C.

In addition to the contract, it is best practice to have ongoing communication with the client to confirm dates of service, fees for service, medications being administered, and any questions you may have before the pet sitting begins and during the pet sitting engagement. You may also want to review the contract from time to time in case any adjustments need to be made.

Veterinary Release Form

You will need your clients to sign a veterinary release form in case there is an animal emergency and you need to take the pet to their veterinarian. Many veterinarians require this documentation before they will agree to an examination and treatment, and clients appreciate this safeguard. (See Appendix D.)

Pet Care Journal Form

You may also find it useful to complete journal forms for each assignment. I use a brightly colored piece of paper for the Pet Care Journal Form, which I leave at each client's home, to chart all their cat's activities and my pet care duties. Having a pet-specific sheet of paper is particularly essential when you need to administer medication as part of your care, because it chronicles what you did on each visit.

On the sheet of paper, I record the daily care I have provided, and I also describe their kitty's adventures, along with any activities or concerns involving the plants and the house. Here's an example of what my journal form typically looks like.

PETS & PETALS JOURNAL

PET SITTING FOR: Wink & Sookie   February 23, 2025 – March 2, 2025

S / M / T / W / TH / F / S /

MEALTIME: *   *   *   *   *   *

CHANGED WATER: *   *   *   *   *   *

PLAYTIME STORIES:
Wink met me at the door followed by Sookie. We had a happy reunion. The kitties led me to their food bowls and ate well. Sookie took her medication in her food well. Wink led me to their play area, and they practiced catching their cat toys. Wink & Sookie enjoyed chasing the laser light, pouncing on catnip bubbles and racing around the house chasing a fleece string. Wink enjoyed sunbaths, and snuggling next to me for pats and purrs. Sookie loved being brushed and brushed. She purred loudly and tapped my hand for more brushings. The kitties enjoyed painting lessons using *Cats Can Paint* online. I am glad you enjoyed their masterpiece that I sent you by text. We had lot of fun visiting and playing.

LITTER: *   *   *   *   *   *
 (Cleaned Daily/Changed)
PLANT CARE: *   *   *   *   *   *

MAIL/NEWSPAPERS: *   *   *   *   *   *

LIGHTS ON/OFF   *   *   *   *   *   *

MEDICINE GIVEN: *   *   *   *   *   *

Sookie 1 tablet in food am only

Please call me or leave a message on my voicemail (at   ) so that I know you have arrived home safely. Thank you for letting me take special care of your cats(s). I hope you have a great trip.

Total @ $ per visit=

My clients enjoy these journals. Some keep them to reread, and they always tell me it makes them smile.

Once you have created or obtained all your forms, along with your business cards and flyers, you are prepared to advertise and market your business. Let's get going!

CHAPTER THREE

ADVERTISING, MARKETING, AND OTHER BUSINESS PROMOTIONS

How can you get the word out about your new professional cat, small animal, and/or plant care service? I have tried many ways of advertising. Here's an overview of what I tried, so you don't have to start completely from scratch. Though none of my attempts were a "cat-astrophe," at the end of the section I will share what worked best—and you may be surprised!

BUSINESSES AND PUBLIC AREAS

With permission, I left my business cards and flyers around places I frequented on a regular basis, such as my school, libraries, veterinary offices, pet stores, health food stores, my gym, local markets, and other bulletin boards I saw that included entrepreneurs' business cards.

LOCAL NETWORKING

I let friends, family, and acquaintances know about my new business, and I asked them to spread the word. I also joined local business organizations like Seacoast Women's Network. I met other professionals, asked a lot of questions, and learned how they ran their businesses.

ONLINE NETWORKING

I added my information to social media sites like Nextdoor.com and Care.com. These sites were easy to access, and soon my business name was shared with my neighborhood.

BUSINESS WEBSITE

Initially, I created a do-it-yourself website through Register.com for free; I just needed to purchase the domain name. This was terrific because I could change the website anytime I wished to update kitty photos and other information. This site also tracked the traffic I received, which let me know the effectiveness of my website.

Later, I upgraded my account to use their professional design team to develop my website further because Google required an SSL (Secure Sockets Layer) for security reasons.

EMAIL

I set up a business address to differentiate my personal email from my business email. I check my business email often during the day to be sure I respond promptly. Whenever a potential client reaches out to me, I get back to them as quickly as possible. This helps ensure that even if I can't fit them into my schedule right now, they have as much time as possible to find someone else. They always appreciate both the referral and the quick reply, which sets a positive note for future business.

SOCIAL MEDIA

Social media can be a great way to advertise your business. Free posts listed on Nextdoor.com, Facebook, Instagram, LinkedIn, BlueSky, and other social media platforms can all serve as effective marketing tools. For instance, some of the towns in my area have pages on Facebook that allow group members to post about their services for free once a month, which can be particularly helpful if you're just starting out.

If you do set up an account on any of these platforms, then you may want to post on or update the site frequently enough to ensure that the people who search for you won't find outdated posts and think you have closed your business. Further, for legal purposes, you would need permission to post anything related to clients, such as photos of the clients' homes or pets. With that in mind, you may wish to post *no* personal material but simply share fun quotes about cats, pet healthcare tips, links to helpful pet websites, and so forth. Since my business is doing very well with just a website and email, I greatly appreciate not having to spend extra time maintaining social media accounts.

CAR MAGNETS, REFRIGERATOR MAGNETS, AND PLACEMATS

I had a magnet made for the side of my car with my business name and logo. It included the words *Pets & Petals—Cat & Plant Care* and my phone number. I left my business magnet on the car when I was parked in a shopping center or driving around town. However, I removed it before I visited my clients' homes, so it would not alert passersby to the fact that the home was unoccupied.

I also pasted my business cards onto magnets that I purchased from Staples. (VistaPrint.com currently offers magnetic business cards all in one.) I shared these magnets with my clients and with local businesses at networking events. Some of my clients still have my original magnets on their refrigerator many years later.

Of course, some people do not like to put anything on their refrigerator, including magnets, so I give those clients placemats for their kitty's food and water. These placemats, which are seasonal, say, "My Pet Sitter Loves Me," and they can be laminated and replaced as needed. As an example, I recently discovered a cute one for the holiday season with a dog and cat dressed in Santa hats whipping up some cookies. The caption read, "Cooking companions stirring up cheer . . . Wags and purrs to all we hold dear!!" The electric beater had the inscription: "My Pet Sitter Loves Me."

This gesture of leaving a placemat shows how much you care about and love their animal companions. You could add your business name and logo to the placemat, too. When friends and family visit your clients' homes and see the placemat, your advertising reach goes even further.

INCENTIVES FOR REFERRALS

As soon as I had a few regular clients, I realized the value of encouraging them to refer other family members, neighbors, and friends to me, and they were more than happy to do so. Today, I am still always grateful for word-of-mouth referrals. As an incentive, I offer my existing clients a finder's fee—one free visit—if I book the new client. This is a win for everyone! Also, to gain more referrals from my veterinarian's office, I randomly drop off sweet treats throughout the year to thank them for their referrals. This keeps me at the top of their mind and brings happy smiles to the hard-working veterinary technicians, office staff, and veterinarians.

CLOTHING ADVERTISING

VistaPrint.com has lots of options to promote your business, such as putting your business name and logo on hats, clothing, bags, snacks and candies, stickers, office supplies, drinkware, and so forth. When I first started my business, my brother gifted me a jacket with my customized Pets & Petals logo. Eventually, it had to be replaced, so my husband gave me a customized Pets & Petals jacket from LogoSportswear.com. It is made of good-quality fabric for use in the rain or cooler weather, and I wear it proudly. Clothes tailored for your business also look official if a neighbor turns up to question your presence at a property, if the police happen to stop by to check the house as requested by the owner, or if there is a problem with the house and you need a professional to stop by.

EVENT BOOTHS

I purchased a booth at several animal-related events, both at my local animal shelter and at wholistic fairs. At my booth, I made connections with potential clients as I sold cat-related items, such as cozy cat beds. These encounters gave me a chance to talk about my cat sitting services and to share my business cards. I also got to meet other pet-loving people, and it was a fun advertising experience.

PROFESSIONAL ASSOCIATIONS

First, I joined the National Association of Professional Pet Sitters (NAPPS), and then I joined Pet Sitters International (PSI). (More information appears in the Reference section of this book.) As I've mentioned, PSI is an educational organization that promotes pet sitters throughout the world. They provide business insurance and hold a yearly conference with informative workshops. PSI members may even be nominated for the Pet Sitter of the Year Award. PSI also manages a forum for members that offers online support for pet sitting dilemmas, and they offer many online classes, trainings, and certifications. Joining NAPPS and PSI helped me from the start because I was able to gain referrals through NAPPS and the PSI Locator. Using this locator, potential clients can input their zip code to view a list of insured pet sitters in their area.

LOCAL MEDIA

I submitted a press release to local newspapers announcing my new business. This was free at the time, and when they published the release, it featured my business and explained where my services would be provided.

COMMUNITY DONATIONS

As another way to advertise, I donated my cat and plant sitting services to be auctioned during local fundraisers. We did note before each auction that whoever purchased or received the certificate would need to be in my service area and their cats would need to be indoors only.

LOCAL PET SITTING LISTS

As I've mentioned, I contacted veterinarians and asked to be included in their list of pet sitters. I did the same for local pet shelters. In particular, I am very grateful to the North Hampton Animal Hospital for all their years of wonderful referrals.

BEST RESULTS

Are you ready to see what worked? Here are the four main ways that I got new clients, listed in order of success.

1.   **Referrals from veterinarians' offices.** Since my veterinarian and their staff knew me already as a pet parent, and they were aware of how well I cared for my own pets, they were happy to refer me to their clients. When they received positive feedback about my work, I moved to the top of their referral list. I received most of my current clients in this way.

2.   **Word-of-mouth referrals from current clients.** As I noted, when current clients refer me to friends, family, and neighbors, if I book the new client, then I offer a free visit to my current client. I thank the current client for recommending me, and I feel honored and appreciated for this support of my growing business. I received many of my current clients in this way.

3.   **People contacting me through my website.** My website provider sends the online requests for service to my business email, so I do not miss a referral. The requests include the potential client's contact information, which makes it easy for me to respond by email. I received several of my current clients in this way.

4.   **Pet Sitters International Locator** (www.petsit.com). When people from my area put their zip code into this locator, my business is listed as an option for them. I have

received several referrals from this site. I also refer other people to this website when they contact me, if I am not a good match, or I cannot fit them into my schedule.

While these are the top four ways I get new clients, all the ideas included in this chapter may work well for you. Most of these ideas do not require much cost, time, or effort, so consider your options carefully and try a few different things at a time. Just be sure to keep track of what works so you know what to keep doing as you move forward!

CHAPTER FOUR

GETTING READY TO LAUNCH

Having a structure in place for essential tasks like scheduling and recordkeeping will help make your business flow smoothly. Now that you're almost ready to launch, the basic tools in this chapter will help make the challenge of running your own business feel a lot less "fur-midable"!

SCHEDULING METHODS AND TOOLS

As clients start to call you, you'll need a method to handle scheduling. Sometimes new pet sitters ask me which works best: setting up scheduling appointments personally, or buying a web-based service to do this? Since I am an individual pet sitter, I prefer to handle each contact personally. Otherwise, unless I constantly update my work assignments and other events in a booking program online, it may look like I'm free when I am not. Then I will end up getting overbooked. To avoid this issue, people contact me directly by cell phone or text, by email, through my website, or through the PSI Locator referral service, and I personally confirm that I am free on those dates.

With that in mind, I also know that many other pet sitters prefer to use an online scheduling service exclusively. Pet sitting software choices include Time to Pet, Easy Busy Pets, and Pet Pocket Book. Many of these options offer other tools as well, such as a single calendar for scheduling, invoices for billing, a way to track how much time you spend on your visits, and a way to upload photos and messages for your clients to review. If you are interested in exploring these scheduling options, this link currently compares more than thirty products to help you determine what might work best for your business: Capterra.com/petsitting-software.

RECORDKEEPING

As a business owner, you will need to keep accurate business records of the following:

- The names and addresses of all clients booked
- The dates of the services provided
- The amount you billed them
- The amount they paid you
- All your expenses (e.g., supplies, gas, and tolls)

I keep a list with the names and address of all my clients in a single file, and I update it each November just before I send out holiday gifts. I store this information not only on my computer but also in an updated printout in case my computer ever crashes.

For each assignment, I write the name of the clients/pets and dates of service and mileage on a physical calendar. This also eliminates the danger of losing my information if there's ever a technical glitch. Then, on my phone's calendar, I input the dates of service again as a backup. The phone calendar also allows me to check my availability on my phone easily when I am out and about. I also note how many visits I complete for each month to see when I am the busiest.

I keep all my expenses in a separate list for tax purposes. I save all receipts for supplies, tolls, and household expenses for my home office, and I give this paperwork to my tax professional each year at tax time. If you are audited, the IRS may want to review your business records, so be sure to keep everything for at least three years. In fact, you should keep all your records for seven years if you filed for a loss or if there are other circumstances that may prompt the IRS to review a longer history of your business financial records.

As you prepare to set up and save your own records, there are a few things to note. First, the IRS allows a deduction for mileage, so it is definitely to your advantage to keep track of that. (See https://www.irs.gov/tax-professionals/standard-mileage-rates.) Second, if your clients pay you through PayPal or Venmo, these firms may report your earnings by sending you and the IRS a 1099. If the clients pay you with a check or with cash, then you will need to create a list of all the money you have received. Payments are discussed in more detail in the next section. The best policy is to be honest in all recordkeeping.

The final—and most enjoyable—records are presented through the Pet Care Journal Forms, which I leave at each client's home. I use these forms to record all the care I provide for the pets and plants each visit. I also use the journal forms as an invoice, which we'll discuss next.

RECEIVING PAYMENTS

I write the fee owed at the bottom of the Pet Care Journal Form, which serves as the invoice, and then I take a photo of that page for my records. I leave a self-addressed envelope for the clients who plan to send me a check when they return.

I also keep track of the payments owed and received on the physical calendar that contains the dates of service, client names, and pet names. As I've noted, many software programs offer invoicing systems that could also work for you.

You will need to set up a separate business checking account to cash any checks made out to your business. Before you start billing clients, you'll want to decide on which payment options will work best for both of you:

- Cash
- Check
- Credit card
- Online PayPal or Venmo (be sure to research any charges and tax implications)
- Other mobile payments, such as Square

My clients have used all these methods except the mobile payments. Most rely on checks, cash, Venmo, and PayPal. The Venmo and PayPal platforms are free to set up, but they do charge a percentage for processing the fee and sending the money to your bank. You will want to factor any vendor fees like these into your budget.

Forbes Advisor has an updated comparison so you can see which payment method is right for your business (www.forbes.com)

advisor/business/paypal-vs-venmo). My clients and I enjoy the ease and convenience of using these payment platforms.

GATHERING SUPPLIES

To help ensure that I always have the supplies I need, I create a pet sitting baggie for each new client's kitty that contains the material that's unique to that particular pet and household.

Here's an example of what I keep in a typical client-specific baggie:

- Their key or passcode
- Their Pet Sitting Information Form
- The Veterinary Release Form

This baggie with all the vital information is essential. When my neighbor, Anita Hubbard, had to cover my clients during an emergency, she greatly appreciated having all this information in one place.

As well, I have a larger pet sitting supply bag with lots of compartments that contains the standard tools of the trade. One of my very talented clients, who is a master quilter, made a beautiful bag for me. I think of this client and her kitties fondly every time I use this stunning carryall, which has just the right number of pockets for all the cat care items.

My bag includes the following:

- Pens
- Kitty litter bags (see discussion that follows)
- Cat litter scoop
- Dustpan and brush
- Laser light
- Catnip bubbles
- Fleece string cat toy (which I bring home and wash in between visits)
- Scissors for opening cat food pouches
- A flashlight
- Paper towels and a hand towel
- A waterproof binder that contains the Pet Care Journal Forms and self-addressed envelopes
- Phone, iPad, or tablet for cat enrichment games

I always try to put the same items in the same compartments so I can grab them quickly for cat care and playtime games. I often feel like the kitties are tapping their paws—*waiting, waiting*—while I make their food or when they want to get playtime started. The more organized I can be, the more quickly and efficiently I can carry out my agreed-upon duties, which also helps the kitties feel well cared for and safe.

As the list notes, I always supply and use my own kitty litter bags purchased from beyondGreen at chewy.com. These plant-based, cat litter waste pickup bags are like dog poop bags, only they are larger and have handles. They are compostable to help our Earth. Even though many of my clients leave plastic bags from the grocery store, I've found that many of the bags leak. Sometimes, a client asks me to take the used kitty litter with me, or I choose to—especially when they are away for many weeks, and I am not taking their trash bins to the curb. I want my clients to come home to a neat, clean-smelling house, which is what the pets deserve, too.

PREPARING FOR SHELTERING EMERGENCIES

There may be rare occasions where it's not safe for the cats to stay in the client's house. For example, I have had to bring kitties to my own home (with the client's permission) after the family's furnace broke while they were away. I am prepared for these situations because I have a guest room in my house where I can keep the kitty safe and away from my own pets. As you finalize your plans to dive into your business, consider where you might take the kitty if a situation like this arises.

Once your business is set up and you've gathered your supplies, it is time to get out there and meet your clients—and their kitties! Let the fun begin!

CHAPTER FIVE

RUNNING YOUR BUSINESS

As I've mentioned earlier, it's really important to make sure you always put your best foot forward and make a "pawsitive" first impression. To help ensure that you don't miss any business opportunities, you should check for phone messages and online messages many times throughout the day and evening. If it's not too late in the day, respond promptly (certainly within twenty-four hours or less). The potential client may be calling several pet sitting agencies, so it can be to your great advantage to be the first person to respond.

This chapter will show you how to interact successfully with new clients in an initial phone interview and during the Meet & Greet. You will learn how to gather important information, such as the cat's history, cat care and house information, trip details, agreed-on job description and duties, daily rates, and payment options. If you decide this client and their kitties are a good match, then you can proceed with getting the Pet Sitting Contract and Veterinary Release Form signed. I will also share how to end a Meet & Greet session, along with follow-up suggestions to confirm the kitty care booking. Not only will these "paw-some" tips help you look, sound, and act professional, but they will also help you ensure that nothing important falls through the cracks.

RESPONDING TO INITIAL CONTACTS

The initial contact from a potential client—and, most important, your response—sets the tone for any future business, and it represents your business brand. Here's the approach I recommend.

- Thank them for reaching out to you.

- If they haven't indicated how they heard about your service, ask. This is great information you can use to assess the effectiveness of your advertising strategies.

- Gather information about the following:

    - Client's name, address, phone number, and email
    - Pet's name
    - Pet's age
    - Pet's breed
    - Ability to stay indoors only
    - Medications
    - Number of visits each day
    - Dates away

- Be sure to confirm that the cat will be comfortable staying indoors while they're away. Some cats find being indoors too stressful, so be sure this kitty has a litter pan and that it can (and will!) manage inside without distress. Otherwise, the cat is likely to pee and poop in an unsuitable area inside the house. Cats who prefer the outdoors may also bolt for the door each time you arrive. I exclusively pet sit for indoor-only kitties.

- Make sure that any other needs are within your level of comfort.

- Advise the client that you provide a minimum service of *daily* pet care for safety and continuity reasons. Some people request a visit only every other day or even just twice a week. I decline these jobs because it may not be safe for the kitty, and I would feel that I was still on duty and responsible for the kitty and their home even on the off days. Daily visits are the standard of practice in the pet sitting field.

- Using the client's address, check the location to see if they are in your service area and if you feel safe about traveling and working there.

- Be prepared to decide if you are offering a discount if the client requests one. I tend to stick to my rates, and this is the consensus from the PSI forum.

- Check your calendar to confirm that you are available.

If you think the client is a good match, then schedule a Meet & Greet at the client's home to gather more information. I do not charge a fee for this Meet & Greet for two reasons: (1) I need this information to take care of their kitty, and (2) based on the meeting's outcome, I may or may not agree to pet sit.

CONDUCTING MEET & GREETS

A Meet & Greet is important because I want to see if the client and their pets are a good match for me. I want the kitties to meet me and see me interacting with their pet parents so they will know I am safe and acceptable in their territory. Here are some tips to make sure each Meet & Greet goes well.

Preparations

Confirm this meeting by sending a text or an email ahead of time to highlight your level of professional communication. Ask the client to respond to make sure the number and/or email address you have is accurate.

Gather the material that you will need to use or share during the meeting:

- Business card and flyer
- Pet Sitting Information Form
- Pet Sitting Contract
- Veterinary Release Form
- Baggie for the key and forms
- Clipboard or leather binder with a pad of paper for taking notes

Plan to arrive at the on-site meeting early or on time. Remember, you are being assessed as well, and establishing trust early on is essential for creating a good working relationship. Give yourself a few extra minutes before the meeting to check out the house and street to see if you feel safe.

Arrival

At the door, introduce yourself briefly, and present your business card. Once inside the house, offer to remove shoes or boots if appropriate. Offer your flyer describing the services your company provides.

First Impressions

Here are some tips that can help you make a great first impression.

- Present as a good listener. (Review the section on great communication beforehand if needed.)

- Determine if the owners wish to tell you all about their kitty before you go through your Pet Sitting Information Form. If so, let the clients lead the conversation, but be sure you get all the information you need before you leave.

- Fill in the Pet Sitting Information Form to confirm the person's name, address, phone number, and email; the pets' names, ages, sexes, and breeds; and the dates of pet care services. By taking these notes, you foster peace of mind for yourself and your client, who is planning to go away and leave the feline member(s) of their family in your capable care.

- Greet each kitty by holding out one finger to the kitty's nose to see if the kitty rubs up against your finger with its mouth. This indicates that further patting contact is allowed. If the kitty moves away, this means you should not pursue this kind of contact at this time. If the kitty moves toward you and likes the contact, then get down low on the floor and sit with the kitty. Be actively involved. For instance, if there is a toy nearby, you may be able to entice the kitty to join you in play. Sometimes, the kitty will be attracted to the reflection on my watch as it dances on the wall, or it might like to play with my shoelace. Many things can become a cat toy! When I play with a kitty who wishes to play, this shows the client how I will be interacting with their cat when they are away.

- Assess the kitty's interactions with you and with its family (and, if there are multiple cats, with each other). Generally, cats are fine when their people are there, but the kitty's behavior may change when their people are away. Noting the cat's personality now will help give you a baseline to check during the pet sitting assignment.

- Have the client describe the cat's likes and dislikes, and any cat games they particularly enjoy. Also, have them describe what a typical day for their kitty would look like.

Contact Information

It's important to have contact information so you can reach out to the client as needed. Here are some particular details you should request.

- Ask if the client will be reachable by text, email, or WhatsApp (if they are traveling internationally) while they are away, and which method they prefer. Ask, "If I can't reach you through your preferred method, what is the next best way to communicate?"

- Sometimes people share where they are going; other times they do not. If they book a long pet sitting request, I do ask where they are traveling because I may need to calculate their time zone in case an emergency communication is needed. I learned to ask this question after I called a new client in the middle of the night because I had miscalculated the time difference between Switzerland and the United States. This was an uncomfortable beginning!

- Ask what day they are leaving and returning. This helps you avoid going to their house when they have not left yet or being there when they arrive home exhausted from their trip.

- Request contact information for their preferred veterinarian and preferred emergency veterinary hospital.

General Cat History

Next, you will want to record the cat's general history.

- Note any information about when the kitties were adopted and other kitty stories that may affect their care.

- Write down the pet's diet, and find out where supplies are located.
- Determine which water the cat prefers (tap or bottled).

- Ask about their typical behaviors and any medical concerns (such as diarrhea; vomiting from hairballs; plant eating, or undigested food; marking with urine or leaking outside the litter pan; and so forth), so you may anticipate these behaviors when their kitties are in your care. Ask about the owners' preferred cleaning supplies and methods for cleaning the floors and rug areas.

- Ask specifics about any medical diagnosis, administering their medications, and any sensitivity to catnip bubbles or plants. I ask this because I may bring catnip bubbles for playtime games. I never bring my own treats or alter their diet in any way because this may cause a medical problem, such as diarrhea or an allergic reaction.

- Practice giving the medication with the client present, if the timing is right for the cat's next dosage. If needed, after the Meet & Greet you should research any required medication and decide if the administration of the medication will be manageable for you. For example, I decline giving insulin

and pills to a cat by mouth because I find the process to be
unreliable, but I will give other medications to cats mixed in
with their food. I refer kitties that need to be given pills by
mouth or that have other medically complicated needs to a
trained veterinary technician. These professionals have special
training and may be available through a veterinary practice to
provide pet sitting care.

- Ask if their kitty likes to be brushed.

- Ask if there are any other pets—such as fish, lizards, hamsters,
  or guinea pigs—in their home, and get the information about
  their specific care.

- Ask and view where the cat carrier is kept, in case you need to
  transport the pet during an emergency.

Paperwork

Ask the client to sign the Veterinary Release Form so that in an
emergency you can notify the client and then transport their animal
to the veterinary hospital. Many veterinarians require a release form
related to care and payment for services rendered. If the client is
reachable, then the veterinarian generally consults with the client by
phone to get approval for treatment and their credit card information.
Be prepared to use your own credit card in case there is a medical
emergency and the client is unreachable. If those situations occur,
make sure you get a detailed receipt so the client can pay you back.

At the Meet & Greet, if it looks like the client will be a good match for me, then I also present them with a copy of the Pet Sitting Contract. When we agree on specific assignment dates, I will fill out the contract and have the client sign it. To ensure that we each have a signed document, I will either share a photo of it with them or I will scan a copy when I return to my office and email it to them. I then file the original in my office. After I complete the first assignment and the client contacts me again by text or email, I confirm the dates and use the text or email as documentation for each pet care assignment. The pet sitting software also has features that easily display and store contracts and the dates of each pet care assignment.

House Details

Usually, the potential client will give you a tour of their house to show you where the cat likes to be, and where pet food supplies, feeding areas, water bowls, and kitty litter pans are. As I have noted, you will want to be sure to find out and note where the cat carrier is kept in case you need to transport the cat during an emergency. Here's a list of other house-related details you'll want to cover.

- Learn about the alarm system, and practice turning the alarm on and off. Write down the alarm code, security password, and alarm company phone number.

- Ask about lights being turned on and off inside and outside the house, as well as any timers.

- Notice any security cameras and motion sensors inside the house. Ask if the cameras and sensors will be on or off during your visits.

- **Very important:** Always ask for and get a key or fob in your hand, and try it out before you leave. Be sure you have two ways to enter the house, such as the garage door code and a keyed door, so you will not need to interrupt your client on their vacation or business trip just because you got locked out of one mode of access. Smart homes usually have a garage code and front door code and fob. At the end of the Meet & Greet, if I think the client and their kitties are a good match, I place the key or fob on a key chain in a baggie with all my new client's pet sitting information. When I get back to my home office, I bring the key or fob to a locked box and catalog it alphabetically by the person's last initial.

- Ask if anyone else has a key or fob to their house.

- Find out who they will line up to cover your visits in case you have an emergency. As an individual pet sitter, you may have your own backup person (and you will want to let the client know about this), but you should also advise them to have a backup person who is ready to help out in case yours is not available. Request that person's name and number.

- Ask about the person to call if there is a house emergency, such as a leaking pipe. Request that person's name and number. This should not be the name of a repairperson; it should be the name of the backup person who will oversee arranging for repairs, letting the repairperson into the house, liaising with the homeowner, and so forth. There may be times when you will need to step in, but having the name of a backup person should keep this to a minimum.

- Ask if you need to be aware of any concerns with their house. Learn where and how to shut the water off. This is invaluable information if a pipe leaks, toilets keep running, or pipes get frozen. Ask about heat and air-conditioning settings, electricity outages, and any contingency plans. For instance, the client may have an emergency generator that goes on automatically, so a power outage is not a concern.

- Ask if anyone else is expected to be at the house, such as cleaning staff, contractors, repair people, relatives, or friends, and decide if you feel comfortable in these situations. Ask if there are any neighbors you need to be aware of.

- Ask if there are any homeowners' association regulations that you will need to observe. For instance, in some cases, the client will also need to give the president of the association your name, as a pet sitter, to keep track of who is entering the homes while the owners are away.

- Ask about plant care, and look at each plant's condition. Ask if they will be watering their plants before they leave and which day of the week the plants get watered. Familiarize yourself with their plants and special light and watering requirements by researching at a nursery and online. I have found that plants can be very communicative, sometimes by wilting or showing yellow or brown leaves to get my attention. I purchased a Dr.meter tester for soil moisture, so I do not overwater the plants. (See the Resources section.) Underwatering is always better than overwatering, since plants can be revived from underwatering. In contrast, plants can drown with too much water, and many do not like to sit in water.

Job Description and Duties

As part of the Meet & Greet, it's really important that everyone is clear on what you will be doing, when, and how.

- For insurance purposes and continuity of care, you may have to explain that you need to be the only person taking care of the cats while the owners are away.

- You may wish to offer to do extra jobs (for a fee or not), such as watering outdoor plants, taking in the mail and packages, taking trash and recycle barrels in and out, putting the lights on and off to make the house look lived in, and refilling the bird feeders (which can be great cat entertainment centers). People really appreciate the menu of services listed on the Pet Sitting Information Form, since they may not think about these extra duties until you mention them.

- Let the client know the amount of time you will spend during each visit. Most pet sitters allot thirty minutes, but I generally spend forty-five minutes to an hour. The client should determine the number of visits they prefer, either once a day or twice a day or more.

Confirmation of a Good Match

Remember, a Meet & Greet is not an automatic agreement to provide services. With all the information gathered and questions answered, I decide if this client still appears to be a good fit for my services. On the rare occasion where I decide that the assignment will not be a good match, I respectfully decline and explain why (e.g., my schedule isn't flexible enough for the times they are requesting, I exclusively take care of indoor-only kitties, I don't take assignments unless they need daily visits, etc.). Alternatively, I conclude the meeting politely by explaining I'll check my schedule once I'm back in my home office, and then I send them a text later that day to decline the assignment. If possible, I refer these clients to another pet sitter, to their local veterinarian (who will likely have a list of pet sitters), or to the PSI locator (www.petsit.com). However, if we do seem to be a good match—which is usually the case—then I proceed with the steps that follow.

Fees and Payment Options

Once I decide to take on a new client during the Meet & Greet, I quote the fee and get verbal agreement that this amount works for them. Always remember that your fees reflect how you value yourself, your time, your experience, and the professional care you are providing.

You will also want to discuss the options for payment. The four options I offer are

- Advance payment during the Meet & Greet
- A check or cash they leave for me to pick up on my first visit
- A check they will mail (I leave my self-addressed envelope)
- A payment through PayPal or Venmo after they arrive home

Because I have never had a problem with a client paying me for my services, I continue to let them decide how they wish to pay. It's understandable that new clients may wish to wait to pay me until after they return home so they can first see that their kitty was well taken care of. Most clients pay in advance or shortly after their return home. As I have noted, I do not offer any discounts or a sliding fee. My rate is based on what I need to receive to make a living and on competitive rates in my area of service. Usually, once a fee is agreed to, I simply present the total cost I've calculated as it appears at the end of the Pet Care Journal Form, but if a client needs a more formal invoice, then I will write one up. In fact, one client traveled so often for work, she submitted the formal invoices to her company, which paid for her kitties' pet sitting visits as one of her benefits.

Final Questions

Before we end the Meet & Greet, I ask if they have any questions for me or if they need to know more about my experience. A good question to end with is, "Are there any final concerns I should be aware of before I go?"

Saying Goodbye

Just as it's essential to make a good impression from the start, it's important to leave on a positive note.

- To begin, I give a personal goodbye-for-now to their kitties.

- I thank the new client and each kitty, emphasizing that I will be happy to take great care of their kitties and look forward to kitty playtimes.

- I restate the kitty and plant care dates. I explain that I will send a confirmation text one week before the assignment begins and that I will text them on the first day I arrive at their home so there is no gap in kitty care.

- I ask my client to text me when they arrive home, so there is no gap in kitty care. (Most clients text me that their kitties came out to happily greet them and all is well.)

- I tell them I will leave a journal form with all their kitties' adventures and the invoice. As you will see in later chapters, I often send a video and photos during the assignment to reassure the pet parent that all is well.

FOLLOWING UP

I follow up each Meet & Greet with a thank-you text. I include the dates of service, and I repeat again that I am excited about the upcoming kitty and plant care visits. I invite them to reach out with questions or schedule changes at any time, and I remind them that I will contact them again one week before the assignment takes place.

CHAPTER SIX

ON THE JOB

Congratulations—you've booked your first pet sitting assignment! This chapter will remind you how to prepare for your first day, and then I will show you what a typical assignment might "paws-ibly" look like. I'll also share how I follow up once my clients return home, plus two important tasks that can help with relationship building: sending gifts and sending condolences.

CONFIRMING SCHEDULES AND MANAGING CANCELLATIONS

As I've noted, one week before the assignment is due to begin, I text the client to confirm the kitty-care dates, and to share any other information or questions I may have. This approach is very helpful in planning my schedule, because sometimes the clients' travel dates have changed but they've forgotten to alert me.

Some clients request a certain time of day for my arrival. Generally, I try to honor these requests, but when I have multiple clients using my services on the same day, it is not always possible. In those situations, I politely explain that each day I am on a different schedule, so my arrival may need to be flexible. I also reassure them that, if that particular time opens up, I will move them into that time slot.

Any policies that you have about schedules and fees—including cancellations—must be put into a written contract and signed by the client up front so there are no misunderstandings along the way. (See Appendix C.) For instance, some pet sitters charge a nominal fee for any cancellations that are not made before a certain window of time, especially if their client is someone who cancels at the last minute on a frequent basis.

I never charge for cancellations or date changes because I believe that, in most cases, people really want to go away, and many of them are disappointed when they must cancel. However, even though I don't require it, several clients have sent me a check to cover a portion of their cancellation dates as a courtesy. This was unexpected and much appreciated! Decide what policies will work best for you, and—most important—make sure they are clear.

A DAY IN THE LIFE OF A CAT AND PLANT CARE PROFESSIONAL

Now that the paperwork's all squared away, let's look at what a day in the life of a cat sitter really "en-tails."

Preparing for the Visit

Before I leave my home office to travel to the first client's home, I complete these preparations.

- I figure out my travel route for the entire day.
- I gather the baggies with the client's key and Pet Sitting Information Form for the homes I will be visiting that day.
- I double-check my pet sitting bag listed in Chapter 4 under Gathering Supplies.
- I pack my Pet Care Journal Forms in the weatherproof binder.

Easing Tensions by Setting Routines

As I've noted, it isn't always possible for me to arrive at each home at the exact same time each day. With that in mind, I try to stick to the same schedule as much as possible. Many cats begin to feel off their routine the moment they see their pet parents' suitcases. Following that situation, they see their family leave without them, and then they discover that a new person has shown up in their house to take care of them. To assist the cats through this stressful time, particularly on the first few days, I try to arrive around the same time on a daily basis. I also follow the same routine during each visit to build the kitties' trust and help them feel safe and secure.

Checking the House Before Entering

I am always alert to my surroundings. If I realize that there are unexpected people in the house when I arrive, then I notify my client and stay outside the house until their identity is known. (A story about this will come later!) If the house looks broken into, I call the client and the police, and then I wait outside for the authorities.

Each time I arrive at the house, I look around and note neighbors, vehicles, and anything unusual. I check for packages and collect the mail. I pay attention to my arrival and departure times. Not only do I want to honor my commitment, but also I am aware that the clients (via cameras or neighbors) and the cat will know if I am meeting my obligations or cutting their visits short.

Greeting the Kitty

Using the safest door for both the kitty and me, which is usually the garage door, I enter the home with my pet sitting bag, ready to block any kitty from trying to escape. I check the alarm system, turn it off, and greet the kitty as I did during the Meet & Greet. I explain what I am doing in their home, where their pet parents are, and when they will return. I use their pet parents' names, and I picture them in my mind, so the kitty can connect them with me.

I bend down to greet the kitties by putting a finger out. If the kitty comes near, I pat it. If the kitty turns away or leaves, I respect this choice and find another way to connect with the kitty. I also confirm that the heat/AC are working by checking the general temperature as I follow the kitty. The kitty will usually lead me to the food preparation area, sometimes with meows.

If I have not seen the kitty at all because it is hiding, then I take time to find it for a greeting. In those cases, I check to see if it is feeling well, and I also make sure that it is in a safe place with access to food, water, and the litter pan. Needless to say, unless there is a specific area that I suddenly need to block off, I leave all of the doors in the home open or shut exactly as the owner has left them, so the kitty doesn't accidentally get trapped in one of the rooms.

Feeding the Kitty and Giving Fresh Water

To serve the cat food, I use a clean bowl or dish that I have washed and dried before each feeding. I prep the food and add any medications and supplements as directed.

If the client has auto-feeders, I check the next time the dry cat food will be distributed. If there is a fountain, I add water to it or clean it completely, as I have been directed by the pet parent.

Some kitties have taught me to turn on the water faucet so they can get a fresh drink.

Some kitties have raised water bowls. It's important to refresh their water bowl daily, not only by washing it but also by wiping it dry to prevent biofilms, which can lead to urinary tract infections and other illnesses.

If there are multiple kitties, I make sure to feed each one. In some households, the kitties eat in separate locations. Some also use a range of different vessels, such as raised food bowls *and* automatic feeders.

Observing the Rules

Kitties like to know the rules so they can follow them to feel safe and secure. This is another reason to gather as much information as possible about the cats, rules, and routines during the Meet &

Greet, and to follow up with the owners as you think of additional questions later. (Just not during their trip unless it's an emergency!) When the rules are clear and followed by everyone, the cat feels the safest.

Here are a few examples. First, the cats may get confused if their pet parents allow them to jump onto the counters—but then I do not. Similarly, they will not understand if the family allows them to drink directly from the faucet—but then I do not.

With that in mind, I usually try to pick the cats up off the counter if I am certain (from my conversations with the clients) that this is breaking a rule. If the cats resist, then I entice them to the floor with a toy, their portion of cat food, or a pet parent approved treat. It's always important to try to remain in the fun pet sitter category as much as possible, so the kitty won't be offended and build up resentment toward your presence.

When I am in doubt about a rule, I remind myself that the cat is probably going to do as it pleases when I am not there, so making a problem about something like walking on the counter—especially for a reactive cat—may be counterproductive. (No pun intended!) If the rules are unknown, then I follow my instincts, always trying to create a positive relationship. I can tell by the look on the cat's face and by the cat's body language if I have made the right choice!

Checking for Surprises and Hazards

During my first visit, I also check around for any other pets that the pet parent may not have mentioned or that have recently arrived. While looking around, I also check for cat hazards like rubber bands, toys with threads or stuffing that have come apart, yarn and strings on the floor, and toys with fishing line or other string features that the kitty could get tangled in. I remove all these toys to a safe place.

I also check for water faucets with a sensor that go on automatically and keep running. I make sure all of the drains are open to prevent the water overflowing. If a kitty jumps up onto the counter and manages to start the water running (even if there isn't a sensor), it may overflow, and unless those drains are open, it can cause a lot of damage.

During each visit, I also check for toxic plants and leaves that have been chewed on. (A link to the ASPCA's list of toxic plants appears in the Resources section.) I move any toxic plants to a location out of the kitty's reach. And whether there are plants or not, I also observe if there is any vomiting or diarrhea. Then I determine if the vomit or diarrhea is new or old. I follow the pet parents' floor and rug-cleaning instructions, and I evaluate how serious the problem seems to be.

A cat vomiting and having diarrhea is not uncommon, but you should be concerned if it is frequent, especially if the pet parent has not alerted you to this issue. (Also see the next chapter on Cat Emergencies.) I make a note of these symptoms on the Pet Care Journal Form, and I try to determine if the vomit is from plant eating or a hairball. If that is not the case and these symptoms continue, then I contact the client to determine if a veterinarian visit is needed.

During two of my overlapping cat sitting assignments, each kitty from a different house vomited its food daily. This really worried me, so I increased my observations of their behavior. I immediately noticed that both cats ate very quickly and regurgitated the food as soon as they were done. To rule out any underlying medical conditions, I consulted individually with each set of pet parents. One client told me the kitty always ate too fast, and they directed me to feed the kitty one teaspoon at a time throughout my pet sitting visit. The other client purchased a slow-feed bowl. Through trial and error, I also discovered that feeding these kitties small amounts of mashed-up wet food throughout my visit and then offering dry food later helped the kitties eat without vomiting.

Cleaning the Litter Box

During each visit, I clean the kitty's litter, noticing any unusual feces or urine, such as a strange color, blood, or spots outside the litter pan. I also notice if the litter pan has not been used. In this case, I try to locate the urine and feces around the house, clean the spots, and alert the pet parents to this behavior in the Pet Care Journal Form for them to address further when they return. If this behavior continues and I cannot locate urine or feces anywhere, then I use the pet parent's contact information to reach out to them to seek advice.

As I finish this task, I remember to sweep anywhere there is cat litter. Clients are very pleased when they come home to a neat house, which reflects my overall attention to detail. The cats also appreciate not having to walk on cat litter specks when traveling to and from their box.

Communicating with the Client

Some clients request daily texts or emails to be sure I was able to enter their house and to let them know that everything is fine with their kitties and their home. As a fun and reassuring surprise, I often send photos and videos of the kitties eating, playing, and lounging in a sunny spot. In each case, I double-check to be sure my communications have been sent. I do not always get a response, but unless I am directly asking a question, no reply is necessary. Many families tell me later that my messages bring them peace of mind because they know their home is safe and their pets are having fun, too.

Some kitties love these photo shoots and pose beautifully.

Sometimes a client who did not request daily communications pops up on my text or email and asks, "How is my kitty doing?" I make sure I am always prepared for this possibility, and I promptly send a description, along with a photo or video I have recently taken. My quick response and photo send valuable reassurance that I am taking excellent care of their animal companions.

Completing Additional Tasks

I complete any agreed-upon jobs, such as watering the plants, taking care of the trash barrels and recycling bins, organizing the mail and packages into neat piles, refilling bird feeders, and adjusting lights and window treatments so the house looks lived in. I note these tasks on the Pet Care Journal Form as well as the cat care I've done.

Playing with the Cats

Playtime is so important, I've included an entire chapter on games and activities I've found that kitties most enjoy! For now, I will provide a general idea of how this special time usually "plays" out.

At each visit, I try to spend quality time playing with the cats who wish to play. Some kitties want to make up their own games, which can be fine, but it's important to make sure they are not destructive or unsafe. For instance, I have taken care of a cat who walked up the client's wooden staircase railing, clawing and scratching it. She had amazing balance! Two other kitties liked to walk along a stair banister that was at least ten feet high. To discourage these behaviors, I tried to steer them toward safer places and activities.

A few kitties prefer to lounge and watch as I present different cat games with the toys at their home. Most kitties prefer to become engaged in the cat games. In fact, some kitties even scratch their claws on their scratching post to let me know they are ready to play!

Some cats start playtime on the floor, while other cats prefer to start up high so they are ready to survey their territory and catch any toy that appears.

Chasing a fleece string or a snake toy is among the favorite games.

Other examples include chasing a laser light, popping catnip bubbles, catching their toys midair, and playing online cat games, all of which I will describe in a later chapter. We also listen to cat relaxation music using online channels such as YouTube and apps such as RelaxMyCat, which has some free offerings and some subscription options.

Some cats love to paint online!

Other cats love to play an online game called Mouse in Cheese.

Some kitties simply enjoy lounging and playing in boxes, a bag, or a tunnel.

Once I find the kitty's favorite thing to do, I repeat this routine each visit. In most cases, when they learn that this playtime occurs each time I visit, they begin to enjoy our time together as much as I do.

Recording Our Daily Adventures

While I am still at the client's home, I record the kitties' daily adventures on the Pet Care Journal Form, along with all the duties I completed and any concerns I may have. I keep the journal entry reasonably short and positive, taking into consideration what I feel that the client would like to read after a long journey home. Here's another sample entry:

> *Charlie ate well and enjoyed finding her treats, which I hid around the house. She loved popping catnip bubbles and chasing her fleece string in between lots of pats and purrs. She chased the laser light in and out of her box. She is such a fun kitty! She loves to play and snuggle and play some more!*

My pet parents enjoy the stories about their pet's antics. This written description reflects my attentiveness and love of their kitty, as well as the care I provide in their home.

Caring for Plants

With research, I found myself up for this challenge. Over the years, I have taken care of some very interesting plants, including a huge Staghorn Fern that lived outside in the summer months and in a warm greenhouse in the winter months. The written instructions left behind by the client simply said to water it every other day. When I could not see where to water it, a quick Internet search alerted me to its root ball, which required watering to be kept moist. To spray or not spray the leaves was another decision I had to make, since the Internet had two differing opinions. Fortunately, the Staghorn Fern did well and survived my care.

Another exotic plant I took care of was an Alocasia Polly plant from Madagascar, which the client called Polly. Polly was not happy unless she received a certain amount of light, moisture, and humidity.

Brushing and Snuggles

Some kitties love to be brushed and to snuggle next to you. I sit down in a chair or on the floor nearby, and I tap my lap a few times to let the kitty know I am available. I also call out their name. If the cat does come over, then I let them smell my hand before giving them any pats. If I am going to offer to brush them, then I let them smell the brush, and I specifically ask them if they wish to be brushed. Kitties will quickly let you know if they approve. I always respect what they tell me, so they do not need to resort to scratching me to get their point across.

Leaving the House

After the kitty has eaten, it has taken the medication and supplements given as directed, it has enjoyed the playtime enrichment games, and it has been snuggled and/or brushed, I let the kitty know I must leave.

I find that generally the kitties are very good listeners and appreciate knowing what to expect.

I know that kitties need twelve to sixteen hours per day of uninterrupted sleep, so I feel fine leaving them to nap, enjoy sunbaths, and follow their usual indoor cat routines.

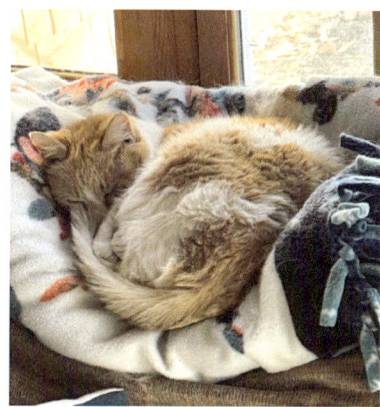

Even when I am booked for an extended assignment, each day I always want to leave the house as neat and tidy as if the clients might arrive home at any moment. Several times, I have had people come back early. Before I go, I dispose of the cat litter in the trash barrel in their garage or bring it home to my trash, since some clients request this. I have an empty kitty litter container in the back of my car for just this purpose.

With the client's house key or fob, baggie with the client's information, my cell phone, my car keys, and my pet sitting supply bag in hand, I make one last check to confirm the following:

- The kitties' food and water are available to them.
- The kitties are content.
- The water faucet and toilet are not actively running.
- The heat/AC are working.

Then I set the alarm system, if needed, and exit.

I discovered a fun way to say goodbye and exit, which I call The Treat Game. This game helps distract the kitty so I can get out of the door as they remain safely inside. To prepare for this game, I confirm ahead of time that the pet parents will allow me to give the cats a few of the treats they usually provide. (As noted, I never bring my own treats because it's unsafe to alter the cats' diets.) If they don't give their cats treats, then I grab a few pieces of their regular dry food instead. (Remember, too many treats or too much food can cause diarrhea.) Then, as I prepare to go, I drop a few treats or pieces of dry food in an area that's far from the door, so that as I leave, the kitty can find the treats by using their hunting skills.

As I drive away, I double-check to be sure the garage door is closed. I am always happy to know another great visit has just taken place.

WHEN THE CLIENTS RETURN

Most people send me a text when they arrive home, which is something we discuss at the Meet & Greet. If I don't hear from them at the end of my assignment, I reach out. If they have extended their stay, or if I have misunderstood their dates, then I need to know that I should keep caring for the kitties until they return.

Once they confirm that they've arrived home, I respond by quickly highlighting their kitty's fun times and thanking them. I also remind them that I've left the completed Pet Care Journal Form for them to review. This "welcome back" communication system also gives the client an opportunity to provide feedback to me, so that in the future, I may correct anything that did not work for them or their kitties.

RECEIVING PAYMENT

As noted, I use the final Pet Care Journal Form to present my total fee to clients, or I prepare a more formal invoice if they need one. I stick to my fee schedule, applying any credit I may have given them in exchange for a successful referral.

For tax purposes, I keep an accurate log of all payments received (income) and any PayPal/Venmo fees (expenses), along with my mileage. If they do pay using Venmo or PayPal, I let them know that I received it and that it is much appreciated. If I don't receive payment after thirty days, which rarely happens, then I send a gentle reminder text. I remind the client that I took care of their kitties on certain dates and the fee owed is _____. I have never had a client fail to pay.

SENDING GIFTS

As part of my business promotions, I love sending holiday packages with chocolates for the pet parents and a cat toy as a surprise gift for the pet. It reminds the pet parents that I love their kitties and value their continuing business relationship with my pet sitting service. If I hand deliver the package, then I put the cat's name on it instead of the client's name, which always brings a smile.

One word of caution: If you choose to hand deliver the package, do not ever use the client's mailbox, which is illegal. A few years ago, before I realized this, I placed the gift package directly in the pet parent's mailbox, and I was given a written citation! Now I send the packages through the postal service, or I drop off the package during a time I am pet sitting at their home. If I have a pet sitting assignment right near the holiday, then I put the package directly under the Christmas tree or leave it for Hanukkah. It is lots of fun to give surprise gifts!

Each year, I have found that the people and their pets love their presents, and this gesture of gratitude is much appreciated. Many of my clients are very generous about leaving tips around the holidays, too, as well as extra-special yummy food, cat-related gifts, and heartfelt thank-you notes, which are all invaluable to me.

I have so much fun picking out the cats' gifts each year. I try to remember if the cat already has a certain toy, and which toys are their favorite. I stay away from toys with bells, eyes that may dangle, long strings, ribbons, or stuffing that may easily fall out. The cats and I really like the safe and durable felted cat toys found at holiday fairs, online, and at local pet stores. Felted mouse toys are always a favorite, as well as toys the kitty can hold in their front and back paws to pummel. It is such a joy to get to know each furry friend, and as I count my blessings, I always look forward to seeing them in the new year.

SENDING CONDOLENCES

One of the hardest parts of my job occurs when a cat I've grown so fond of passes over the Rainbow Bridge. Saying goodbye to the kitty and—if I am invited—attending their euthanasia appointment is always a difficult time. I try to comfort the pet parents as we tell stories and reminisce about their kitty's life. If I have a photo, I send it to the pet parents at the time of their cat's passing (or sometime later), along with a personal note in a cat loss grief card expressing my condolences. I know that even months later, their animal companion is still very much on their mind and greatly missed. I have so many wonderful memories of my kitty clients, and I continue to think of them often, even after they are no longer with us.

CHAPTER SEVEN

CAT-RELATED EMERGENCIES AND SPECIAL NEEDS

Thankfully, over the past thirty years, I have not had many cat-related emergencies, but I believe it is important to keep learning as much as we can about medical and behavioral concerns for cats. Not every day on the job will run "purr-fectly." We need to be prepared when an emergency arises, and we need to have protocols we can follow to remain calm and relaxed while taking care of the kitty and communicating with the pet parents. As I have noted several times, pet first aid classes are essential for pet sitters. Even if you have taken one of these classes in the past, I highly advise you to take refresher courses periodically to keep up to date on treatments for medical concerns.

This chapter provides a general overview of some of the medical and behavioral problems you may encounter, along with some suggestions for how to address them. I will also share what symptoms you should watch for if you are scratched or bitten, and, if the client's cat needs treatment, how you can prepare to transport it to the vet. Please note again that this is general advice only; it will not serve as a replacement for veterinary or medical advice, and you should always reach out to professionals as needed. We will wrap up the chapter with advice on caring for aging cats, a wonderful group of felines that may develop their own unique needs.

MEDICAL-RELATED ISSUES

For new clients and for those I have not worked with in a while, I always get a description of their kitty's most recent behaviors related to vomiting of food and plants, diarrhea, litter box and grooming habits, and updated medications and supplements. I confirm the name, address, and phone number of their current veterinarian, and I get a signed Veterinary Release Form if they have changed practices.

Vomiting

Vomiting is actually a pretty common behavior in cats. Cats may vomit due to any of the following reasons:

- Stress
- Eating plants (even if the plants are nontoxic)
- A hairball
- Long gaps between meals
- Eating too quickly, which triggers a stretch reflex in their stomach
- Eating foreign objects that become stuck or cause damage to their GI tract, such as elastics, strings, dental floss, parts of toys

- Eating too many treats or a different food
- Parasites
- Inflammatory bowel disease
- Constipation

When I see that the cat has vomited, I try to identify what exactly the kitty has expelled, and I write this on the Pet Care Journal Form. If the vomit is not clearly due to fur, food, or plant material, then I take a photo, since this may signal a more serious problem. If it is clearly due to plant material, then I assess the situation to see if the plant is listed as toxic. (A link to the ASPCA's list of toxic plants appears in the Resources.) I remove the plant from the kitty's reach if necessary.

If the vomit contains catnip or safe grass greens, I am less concerned, because I know cats often vomit this up to clear their system. If the cat has vomited digested or undigested food bits, then I try to determine if the kitty waited too long between feedings or ate too fast. In those cases, I adjust the time of my arrival and use a raised bowl, a slow feeder, and/or a slower feeding method, such as offering a teaspoon of mashed-up food every five to ten minutes, to help the kitty digest the food better. In all these situations, I clean the vomit up with solutions previously approved by the pet parent.

Exhibiting Other Symptoms

If I observe frequent vomiting, diarrhea, or blood in the cat's stool, I don't panic immediately, because these symptoms could be due to stress, eating too many treats, or the ingestion of a toxic substance, like a plant or their own fur that has turned into a hairball. As a first step, I usually check the house for any other hazardous materials that the kitty may be exposed to. After that, I record the symptoms on the Pet Care Journal Form and decide if I need to communicate with the pet parents to determine the next step for taking care of their kitty.

As a caring professional cat care provider, I always make the kitty's comfort and health my primary concerns. In these situations, I ask myself, *"What would I do if my kitty was presenting in this way?"* Here are symptoms that always prompt me to reach out to the pet parents to seek permission for a veterinary visit:

- Allergic reactions
- Bleeding
- Bite wounds that aren't healing
- Breathing problems
- Convulsions
- Pain
- Seizures
- Serious injuries

If the pet parent cannot be reached, I call the veterinarian's practice or (if after hours) the emergency veterinary hospital or urgent care for pets to seek professional advice. It is essential to keep a close eye on the kitty so you can describe all their symptoms.

As part of my business operations, I am always ready to transport the kitty to a veterinary practice as needed. I make sure I know in advance where their carrier is, and I also keep a carrier in my car as a backup. Be sure to bring the signed Veterinary Release Form with you to the practice. I will share more helpful tips about vet visits and cat transportation later in this chapter.

Urinating Outside the Litter Pan

As I mentioned in the previous chapter, during each visit I check to see if the kitty is using the litter pan daily for both urine and stools, which is normal behavior. Most kitties urinate and defecate at least once a day. I also notice if the kitty is just walking around in the litter (not using it at all). Of course, if there is more than one kitty under my care, it can be hard to figure out which one is not using the box.

If you notice urine outside the litter box or smell urine in unusual places, these could be signs of marking behavior, or a urinary tract infection. Sometimes cats mark their territory to protect it from another cat in the house or from cats outside their window; sometimes they just do it to help themselves feel safe.

On the second day of one of my assignments, I noticed the kitty had not used the litter pan. This could be a symptom of a urinary blockage, so I searched the house for urine spots. I noticed a bed downstairs with a pillow and a bedspread that had a urine smell. I was glad the kitty was peeing, but I was concerned about where he was peeing. I cleaned up this area and closed the door to this bedroom to help retrain the kitty to use his litter pan. Fortunately, he cooperated and, happily for everyone, he used his litter pan the next day. I noted this behavior on the Pet Care Journal Form in case any follow-up steps were needed.

If the kitty is urinating outside the litter box and this is unusual behavior for this particular cat, then I clean the urine up, noting if there is any blood in the urine, and I document this behavior. Sometimes older kitties with compromised kidneys urinate outside the litter box, and the pet parent is aware of this. Some of my clients provide puppy pee pads to place around the litter box or in certain areas where the kitty tends to urinate.

If I notice other symptoms in addition to the urination issues—such as the kitty not eating or acting lethargic—then I notify the pet parents immediately to see what they suggest.

Overheating

Cats were originally desert animals, which is part of the reason they love to lounge around in the sunshine. Their temperature runs between 101°F and 102.5°F, which is a bit higher than ours. Be especially alert for symptoms of overheating in certain breeds like Persian cats, obese and senior cats, kittens, and cats with underlying heart and lung disease, because they are particularly vulnerable to heat-related conditions.

Heat stroke symptoms include the following:

- Bloody diarrhea
- Collapse
- Difficulty breathing
- Drooling
- Excessive panting
- Increased heart and respiratory rate
- Mild weakness
- Seizures
- Temperature of 104°F or above
- Vomiting

If you notice any of these symptoms, contact the pet parents and the veterinary hospital, and—as directed—proceed to the veterinary hospital immediately.

Transporting Cats to the Vet

I have transported several kitties to their veterinarian for a variety of reasons. One client even paid me to take their ailing cat to the vet for them because they had a full day of meetings, even though technically they were not away, and I was not on a pet sitting assignment for them.

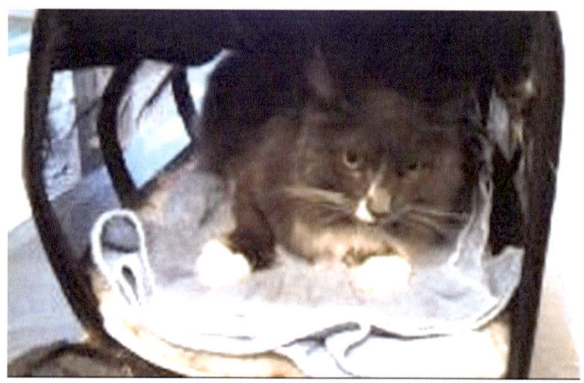

Another kitty had renal bleeding that I noticed during my assignment. At the emergency veterinary hospital, I learned that she had a urinary tract infection. This was a serious illness, and my clients (both human and kitty) were very much appreciative of my intervention.

In another situation, I transported a kitty to the veterinarian because electrical tape was stuck to the kitty's front paw after he had an adventure involving a treasure hunt in his attic. The veterinarian had a special liquid solution that removed the tape immediately. I was so grateful—and so were his pet parents!

In each of these cases, I made an appointment with their regular veterinarian or called ahead to an emergency veterinary clinic. At the practice or clinic, I presented the Veterinary Release Form and gave the professionals as much information as I could about the kitty's symptoms and behaviors. I stayed with the kitty in the exam room to reassure it, and I waited for the veterinarian to diagnosis the problem, contact the pet parents, and proceed with the treatment plan to help the kitty feel better. Sometimes I paid for the veterinary care and was reimbursed by the clients later, and other times the pet parents provided their credit card information to me or the vet for these services.

As some of you may already know, sometimes the hardest part of a trip to the vet is getting the cat in the carrier. Here are some tips that may help.

1. Encourage the kitty to move into the bathroom or a room without hiding spots. If the kitty has the run of the house or is hiding under a bed, this may lead to a chasing game that is very upsetting both for the kitty and for you.

2. As gently and quickly as possible, scoop the kitty up by scruffing them by the neck (gathering the fur around their neck area) like their mother did when they were a kitten to transport them.

3. Support their back paws and put them headfirst or back feet first into their carrier.

During this process, talk to them calmly. Softly explain what you are doing, and gently describe where you are going to help them feel as calm as possible.

BEHAVIOR-RELATED ISSUES

Not all of the challenges you may face are due to physical issues. In this section, I'll share some of the behavior-related issues I've encountered, along with suggestions about how you may approach similar situations on the job.

Escaping from the House

Another emergency you may need to deal with is having the kitty escape from the house. Even if you take care of indoor cats only, the kitty may still escape.

I have had three kitties escape. One was definitely smarter than I am to begin with. You will know when you meet a cat like this! In this case, I was sure that I had closed the screen door, but after preparing food for the kitties and cleaning their litter, I noticed that one kitty was on the outside of the screen door looking back in at me! I was so alarmed, I went right outside to pick up the kitty and bring him inside. Crisis averted—but I was shaken and remained on high alert for future cats and their possible escape strategies.

On another occasion, in another home, I moved the cat perch up to the slider door so that the kitties could be comfortable and watch the wildlife outside. When I returned the next day, the slider door was open. It seemed like the cats had gone outside, but they were back inside when I arrived. I was confused and alarmed, but also grateful that both kitties were safely inside their house. I moved the perch away from the slider door, wondering how on earth they could have unlatched and pushed that door open. After the assignment, the clients read my report about it on the Pet Care Journal Form, and they explained that a neighbor had been letting the cats in and out during the day. Phew! I was glad that mystery was solved, and the cats were safe.

Another time, I realized that the kitty had gotten out through a loose screen in the basement. I called and called the kitty in the fields nearby, and I tried to entice him back inside the house with kitty food. Nothing worked. This was a long and worrisome pet sitting week. Fortunately, a relative stopped by, and she was able to coax the kitty back into the house. Now I always check basement screens and open windows around the house for possible cat escape routes.

Getting Stuck

As I've noted, I don't bring catnip or treats to the kitties anymore due to the risk of digestive upset. However, before I adopted that practice, I once used a plastic grocery store bag to carry loose catnip in to share with some of my feline clients. A curious kitty was so enticed by the catnip, he put his whole head into the bag. Somehow his head got caught in one of the handle loops, and he raced around the house trying to get free while the bag acted like a sail behind him. He finally stopped racing around and hid under a bed, where he immediately peed to highlight his upset. I was able to safely cut the bag from around his neck—and clean up the puddle under the bed—but the poor little scared kitty! I felt terrible and learned my lesson: Never use plastic grocery store bags as carriers on the job.

Hiding

I always locate the kitties I am caring for each day. Most cats love company, but some cats do not, and they feel stressed sharing their home with an unfamiliar person. However, as a pet sitter who is responsible for the welfare of the cat, is imperative for you to see the kitty and check for any health concerns.

You never know where you will find the kitty. I am always determined to locate the cat for their safety and my peace of mind. Once I looked and looked, upstairs and down, only to find the kitty in a sink cabinet locked with childproof fasteners! I quickly opened the cabinet and freed the kitty.

Another time I was also searching upstairs and down, calling the kitty's name with no success. Eventually, when I decided to look up, I spotted the kitty on a high shelf above the refrigerator. That kitty certainly must have been laughing as I was frantically calling, looking all around, and passing his hiding spot time after time. So, look into cabinets, look up, and be sure that during each visit, you have eyes on the cats!

Most cats are good at hiding—and finding them can take extra time. They're also quite skilled at picking new hiding spots before my next visit.

Some cats are shy and get stressed if I approach them or stay too close. Fortunately, most kitties can be coaxed out from hiding with cat treats, kibble, and a calm demeanor. I offer kind, whispered words to make them feel safe. I also play cat relaxation music and watch their response to assess if the kitty would like further interactions. Then, if they come out, I try to return to business as usual: I engage them in cat games if they're willing, or I sit nearby for a visit and a chat if they're not. Sometimes I can even take a photo of these sweet kitties.

In more extreme cases, once I've viewed the kitty, the best course of action is to leave it alone and hope that the next visit is less stressful. Signs that the cat does not want to be approached include the following:

- Big pupils (meaning *I am scared*)
- Hissing (meaning *Give me space*)
- Lip licking, overgrooming, or pulling their fur out (meaning *I am stressed*)
- Yawning (meaning *I am trying to relax my body because you are stressing me out*)

In those cases, I recommend that you move slowly away from the kitty and leave it alone. You can always try again on your next visit.

Becoming Aggressive and Territorial

Most of the cats I have taken care of throughout these many years are delightful. We love each other, and we have harmonious visits. There are, however, cats who simply will not accept me into their home.

For instance, in one household, there were two kitties who were antagonistic toward each other. The cats shared a space where they had to pass each other often. Initially, at the Meet & Greet, I thought it unusual that one of the two kitties climbed up and sat in my lap for pats. However, both cats and I seemed to get along well, so I accepted the assignment.

When I arrived for the job, both kitties were initially welcoming, and one climbed up on the stove counter area while I made her food. I encouraged her to climb down to the floor, and we seemed to get along fine. After she ate a plate of special cat food, she enjoyed painting online and chased some of her toys. The other kitty stayed in his room, and I visited with him there. It was a brief, two-day assignment, and I experienced no issues.

To my great surprise, the next time I cared for them for an extended trip, it turned out to be a very different experience. I entered as usual, and the less reclusive kitty ate her special diet. Then I thought she would enjoy the cat enrichment games she had enjoyed previously.

Unfortunately, the kitty had another game she wanted to play, which apparently was called "You be the prey, and I will stalk and scratch your leg." As I was sitting on the couch, the kitty looked at me, came near me, and scratched my leg. This was not a tap. This was an offensive scratching gesture. I was startled and moved away, protecting my legs. I talked with the kitty calmly, wondering, *What is going on?*

As I looked at the kitty, I actually felt scared, because she seemed determined to stalk and swat at me. I gathered my things and walked quickly out of the door . . . with her running behind with big eyes—yowling!

This house had cameras, so the video must have been quite a sight. I was afraid to enter the house again, and I wracked my brain as I tried to understand this kitty's aggressive behavior and figure out ways to get along with her. Since the clients were far away and not able to readily return home, I decided to protect myself on my next visit by wearing knee-high boots, a long coat, and gloves, even though it was a hot week in the summer.

The kitties were fine when I arrived, and they behaved normally while I was making their food, but right after the kitty that had been aggressive ate, she turned back into a predator. I had to work around her eating area to be able to clean the litter, and while I did so, I remained on high alert for an attack. Then I fed and checked on the other kitty, who was scared and hiding out under the bed because he had been swatted by this kitty as well. Each day I worked quickly to change their water and clean both litter boxes before the kitties were finished eating. Then I ran to the porch and out the door.

One day when I was ready to leave, the kitty was on a perch right by the door. I passed quickly by the perch, using my cat bag to protect myself and avoid a swat. As I closed the glass door behind me, I heard a loud yowl! The cat was actually lunging and throwing herself at the glass door, as if she wanted to get me! I was very upset because I was afraid the kitty would hurt herself.

Since things were not getting better, I did more research to try to understand what was causing her behavior, and to find a way to create more harmonious visits for us all. According to the Cornell Feline Health Center's website, which I've included in the Resources section, there are many different causes of aggressive behaviors, which can be a common problem in cats. To prevent injury (feline or human!), it's important to recognize these signs of aggression and fear.

- Dilated pupils (aggression or fear)
- Ears flattened backward on the head (aggression)
- Ears flattened and held backward (fear)
- Whiskers flattened or pressed downward onto the face (fear)
- Tail held erect with hairs raised and an arched back (aggression)

- Tail closely wrapped or tucked under the body (aggression)
- Head held upward while lying prone (aggression)

The Cornell Feline Health Center also lists the following types of aggression:

1. **Play Aggression:** Cats that have not had littermates to teach them about biting and scratching too hard

2. **Fear Aggression:** Cats that encounter an unfamiliar person, animal, or noise or that are exposed to an unpleasant experience, such as a trip to the veterinarian

3. **Petting-Induced Aggression:** Cats that suddenly become aggressive when being petted

4. **Redirected Aggression:** Cats that are excited by something they cannot directly respond to (e.g., a stray cat they see outside the window, a loud noise, or an upset with another pet in the house), so they lash out at a person or another pet instead

5. **Pain-Induced Aggression:** Cats that are in pain and want to avoid touch, movement, or certain activities that may cause more pain

6. **Status-Induced Aggression:** Cats that block the doorway or hide under a table waiting to ambush or swat at other cats or people to establish social dominance

7. **Maternal Aggression:** A nursing mother cat that becomes aggressive toward people or animals that approach her

8. **Inter-Cat Aggression**: Male (and some female) cats that become aggressive toward other male cats as they approach social maturity between two and four years of age

9. **Territorial Aggression:** Cats that defend their territory and become aggressive toward new cats, people, or other animals if they smell different

It remained a mystery as to precisely what set this kitty off. However, based on my research, it appeared to be territorial aggression toward me, and status-induced aggression toward the other resident cat. The aggressive cat primarily acted out after she ate. She was friendly when I entered, allowing me to prepare her food and give her a pat. I could only conclude that since cats are highly sensitive and count on routine, she was suffering stress and anxiety from the general situation, which was leading to territorial behavior as she sought to protect her perceived safe space. I realized this was a complex concern that was likely exacerbated by my twice daily visits. She was clearly displaying not only fear but also defensive aggression, and she was treating me as a perceived threat from which she could not escape. I observed a combination of defensive signals, such as flattening the ears and tucking the tail, and aggressive signals, such as hissing and swatting.

By watching the cat's body language, I learned that I had only about fifteen minutes to be in her territory before she would act aggressively. I decided that in order to try to alleviate the kitty's stress, my best plan was to avoid her as much as possible throughout my assignment and hope she would calm down. All I could do was quickly enter, provide kitty care, and leave before the kitty finished her meal.

Obviously, this was not the level of service I was used to providing, since it was so quick and did not offer any typical interactions or playtimes. During this period, her pet parents asked how it was going. Initially, I sent photos to accent the positive aspects of the visits, but I also asked them to review their camera footage to see more accurately what was happening. I planned to discuss her behavior further when they arrived home. The pet parents were perplexed and stated that they had not seen this behavior before. They also thought the kitty was acting territorial.

We discussed alternatives for their future pet sitting needs, such as a kennel, since their kitty would not feel the need to protect her territory in a neutral environment. The pet parents did contact me a few months later for pet sitting services. However, I declined further pet sitting for their kitties, since I did not want to upset their kitties and reexperience this stressful situation.

After this experience, I was on high alert for signs of a territorial cat, and soon after, I met another one. Initially, during the Meet & Greet, the client and kitty seemed fine—until the kitty went under the dining room table and hissed and swatted at her pet parent's leg! Looking back now, I realize that was a message we should have listened to!

I had not seen this scenario before—a cat acting aggressive to its own person—and we were all perplexed and a bit unnerved. As a precaution, I decided to try a brief visit to see how we would get along. The kitty was fine and playful, so I agreed to a longer visit and booked another assignment.

During the assignment, the kitty became aggressive with me. She stalked me and yowled as I was putting her food onto her placemat, changing her water, and cleaning her litter. Her big eyes and body language let me know that I needed to protect myself. I put her cat tunnel and my cat bag between us, so she never had the opportunity to make contact.

As I considered this situation, I wondered if I was bringing other cats' smells into her house. Could that be what was precipitating her aggressive behaviors? Unfortunately, this unpleasant behavior continued even though I used a clean cat bag and only her own litter scooper and cat toys.

Although we never pinned down the exact issue, I soon received evidence that the general problem was related to me. One day when I was there caring for the cat, I met a contractor who had been doing work there for several days before I arrived. He mentioned that the cat was always fine with him. In fact, he was very surprised to see the cat hissing and yowling at me.

When the pet parent arrived home, I told her that I needed to return her key and could not take future assignments. We discussed the cat's behavior and my attempts to calm her down. I noted that her kitty was not comfortable with me and was clearly upset with me being in her house. I explained that since she was so unhappy in my presence, it would not be fair to leave her again with someone with whom she was not comfortable.

The pet parent was understanding. She made plans to hire a pet sitter who did not have pets and who would not be caring for other animals during the assignment. That would eliminate the possibility of introducing the smell of other animals into the house, in case that was what was upsetting the kitty. I wish that I could have assisted, but this kitty clearly knew what she wanted and how to communicate her needs!

Dealing with Biting and Scratching

While we're on the subject of aggression, let's talk about biting or scratching, which can be caused by a variety of factors. As we've seen, when kitties are unwell, feel they need to protect their territory, or are trying to get a point across, they may try to bite or scratch to protect themselves or to indicate they wish to be left alone.

As with most things, an ounce of prevention can be worth a pound of cure. Here are some ways you can try to avoid or address this behavior.

- Ask clients to ensure that the cats' claws are trimmed regularly for their health and your safety.

- When a cat is trying to bite or scratch, redirect their attention to a cat toy to satisfy their hunting instincts and get their energy out.

- Point their attention toward a scratching post as an outlet for their behavior.

- Watch for cat body language that lets you know they have had enough of your patting or brushing them or that you are too close to them. Tell them you understand, and stop your behavior that is agitating them.

- Put an object in front of you and the kitty to prevent contact.

- Discuss any behavioral concerns with the pet parents when they arrive home—or immediately, if necessary.

The Cornell Feline Health Center also notes that if you encounter a cat fight, you should never put your hand or any part of your body between cats that are fighting. Using a barrier like cardboard, a cat tunnel, or a baby gate to separate aggressive cats is safer.

Unfortunately, even with these precautions, there may be times when a cat successfully lashes out and harms you. In those cases, it's important to know that your health may be at risk. Cats have very sharp teeth and claws that can penetrate your skin deeply and expose the wounds to bacteria. Before we move on, let's quickly look at what steps you should take, what symptoms you should watch for, and what treatment you should seek. (Please note again that these tips should never replace the advice of a medical professional; always seek medical advice if needed.)

To treat a cat bite or scratch that is not infected, you can follow these initial steps.

- Wash the wound thoroughly with soap and water (up to five minutes).

- Clean your hands thoroughly before and after attending to the wound care.

- Apply a dry sterile dressing to your wound, and change it as needed.

- If your wound is bleeding, put a clean, soft cloth on the area. Apply firm pressure until the bleeding has stopped. This could take up to five minutes. Do not remove the pressure to look at the wound during this time.

- Apply an antibiotic cream to the wound, and leave it uncovered to heal.

The first signs of infection may appear within a few hours, so look at your hands, tendons, and joints, which are high risk. Make sure that your tetanus shot is up to date, and seek medical treatment right away if it is not. You should also seek medical treatment within eight hours to decrease the risk of infection if any of these signs are present:

- A bite that is deep or severe
- A red line going up your arm from the wound toward your heart
- Red lumps or streaks
- An elevated temperature of 100.4 F (38C) or higher
- Flu-like symptoms: chills, headache, swollen lymph nodes, fatigue
- Tenderness or pain
- Redness, swelling, and or/heat at or around the site
- Trouble moving the body part
- Pus: white, yellow, or other-colored thick fluid

Again, it's *extremely* important to take these situations seriously, because you may need stitches, medication, or even hospitalization. The bacteria injected by a cat bite can include strains common in animals that can be hard to treat, even with antibiotics.

AGE-RELATED CONCERNS

On a happier note, I love taking care of kitties of all ages, and I find that very senior kitties are especially loving. I feel honored that they allow me to take care of them in their golden years. With that in mind, pet sitting for very elderly kitties—cats ages 18 to 22 (which translates to 88 to 104 in human years)—requires a whole different level of care that pet sitters need to learn about and provide.

Here are some of the issues you may encounter.

- The very senior kitty may sleep a lot more.
- Kitty games may not be of interest or may be played in a more observant way.
- The kitty's movements may not be as fluid.
- The kitty may vocalize more.
- The kitty may need a smaller area to maneuver in.
- The kitty may have more accidents, due to thyroid or kidney concerns.
- The kitty may not see and hear as well as they used to.
- Some kitties need help climbing onto a bed and may require steps.

In my experience, most very senior kitties are wonderful. Some snuggle next to me for pats, and others let me pick them up to put them onto their bed or perch for a sunbath. Here are some adaptations I make to ensure that these seniors are comfortable.

- I try to be flexible during their mealtime. The pet parent may describe them as finicky eaters, liking one food and eating it enthusiastically one day, then rejecting that same food when it is offered again. In that case, it can help to make sure the client has left multiple food options for you to offer. (Of course, some senior kitties continue to be great eaters even into their golden years of age twenty and up.)

- I walk slowly and keep myself in their sight line to help them feel more secure. I sit nearby the very senior kitty, offering pats, helping them up onto furniture, and giving them breakfast in bed as directed by the pet parent.

- I refresh their catnip toys by crumbling up the catnip inside, so the kitty can sniff it. Most senior cats find this enjoyable, and it keeps their senses stimulated.

- I follow the kitty's lead, learning what they like best to make them feel comfy and cozy.

- I respect the senior kitty's nap times and try to visit when they are awake.

- I discuss contingency plans with the owners in case of emergency, including instructions for the sad possibility that the kitty might pass while the owners are away.

One lovely, very senior kitty I care for loves her naps, and she enjoys snuggling under the covers. She allows me to pick her up and put her on the bed, and then she wants me to cover her up from head to tail, tucking her in. So sweet!

Sometimes it is also necessary to make temporary alterations to the house to keep these kitties safe. For instance, this kitty's pet parents took steps to block off the access to their second floor since she is not steady walking anymore, and they were concerned she would fall down the stairs. Imagine my surprise when I arrived on one visit and could not find the kitty downstairs! When I looked upstairs, I discovered that the determined kitty had slid through a small opening between the stair rails so she could go upstairs, where she was sleeping on one of the beds. I talked with her, picked her up, and then carried her downstairs to her bed. I created additional temporary blocks to the stairs for her safety. Her pet parents were very appreciative.

Now that you've got a better handle on how to manage emergencies and special situations with your feline clients, let's take a look at some of the challenges you may face as you care for their homes.

CHAPTER EIGHT

HOUSE-RELATED CHALLENGES

In some cases, dealing with a client's home maintenance issues can be even more "purr-plexing" than taking care of their kitty! I've found that when I am new to the house and/or the house is new to my client, unexpected situations may arise. The stories I share in this chapter should help you tackle similar challenges if they occur while you are pet sitting.

RESPECTING THE CLIENT'S POSSESSIONS

As a pet sitter in the client's home, I am responsible for making sure everything in the house is kept as my client left it. As you may know, people usually have their house set up in a way that they and their cats like, so ideas about moving anything around are off limits and unwelcomed. Consequently, I am very careful to avoid moving anything in the client's house, unless it is hazardous to the cat.

For example, in my own house I do not mind if cat toys are left out on the floor, but some clients like to have everything put away. Even if I would like to make a point (e.g., *See how much fun we had while you were away*, or *Your kitty likes to play with their toys in between my cat care visits*), I do not redecorate their house with cat toys left out on the floor.

I treat each client's home with extra care, leaving everything as they have it. I do not open drawers, closets, or closed doors. Once I accidentally broke a cat food plate, so I replaced it. Be honest with the client if you do break something, and replace it or offer to do so. This is essential to sustain a trusting relationship. You can check with your insurance to see if a claim would apply if the item is expensive.

Most people notice when something in their home has been used, moved, or rearranged in some way. Several of my clients' homes have cameras. Some clients let me know they have cameras or may have an indoor camera installed in the future. Others do not let me know. Once I looked straight into an Owl camera—not knowing what it was until I googled it much later!

Sometimes the clients use cameras to monitor how much their cat is eating, and to watch the comings and goings of the cat as it moves around their home. Whenever I'm on the job, I try to act as if I am always on camera. I think about how my actions would be perceived by the pet parents as I interact with their cats and do my daily pet-care chores.

Remember, the cats are always watching you! Even though cats do not use language like we do, they show their feelings of contentment or distress clearly when their pet parents return home.

CLOSING WINDOWS

There are a few exceptions to leaving everything as the client left it. For instance, what if a client has left their first-floor windows wide open during the summer months? I try to view this situation from a cat and house safety point of view and make the best decision. Rain may come in, or the cat can become extremely interested in a creature outside and push the screen out, or an intruder could take advantage of an opened window. Depending on the weather, I will close the windows and then, if I'm questioned about it later, explain my concerns.

ADDRESSING NO HEAT IN THE HOUSE

One cold winter, during an ice storm, I took care of a kitty in an office where the kitty was temporarily staying. When I arrived, I discovered that the heat had gone off. The kitty was cold, the office was cold, and the alarm was going off due to a dead battery.

With permission from the pet parent, I contacted the alarm company, and they told me how to deactivate the alarm by disconnecting the wires to quell the noise. But it was still extremely cold. Even though kitties have fur, they can still suffer from hypothermia.

After contacting the pet parents again, I was able to bring the kitty to my own home to stay warm. Fortunately, as I've mentioned, we have a guest room in our house for kitty emergencies. The sweet kitty snuggled into a warm bed in our quiet house, and he enjoyed his stay with us until his pet parents arrived home.

Another time, I observed that the thermostat in the clients' house was dropping below 60°F. I immediately contacted the pet parents to alert them to the problem, and they gave me permission to bring their twenty-year-old cat to my house, where she enjoyed my guest room for the rest of the clients' vacation. The client took separate steps to get their furnace repaired before their return, but we agreed that it was better for me to continue to keep the cat at my home, where she was warm, well cared for, and loved.

DEALING WITH FROZEN PIPES

Situations when the heat goes off are concerning, but what about frozen pipes? If you live in warmer climates, you do not have to worry about this, but at low temperatures in northern states, especially in homes with uninsulated pipes, the water may freeze—bursting the pipes and flooding the house. As I mentioned earlier, at the Meet & Greet I always find out where the water shutoffs are, and how to use them. I also request the name of a knowledgeable backup person in case of an emergency at a client's house. However, the following story shares how I first learned to do this—almost the hard way!

During one icy-cold, sub-zero January day, I contacted all of my clients to ask if—as a precaution—I should leave their cabinet doors open and keep the water taps slowly dripping, which is a traditional way to prevent frozen pipes. Some people thought this was a good idea, while others decided their house would be fine without any special preparations.

During this cold snap, I was in a house where I had been running the water once a day, so I did not think any extra precautions were necessary. However, on the last day of my pet sitting assignment, no water came out of the faucet in the left sink, which is the one that I had been using daily. The water faucet in the right sink was working, and all the other faucets throughout the house were fine. The pipe that I had been using daily had frozen overnight! I contacted the backup person, who oversaw any house problems, and left a voicemail about this predicament.

I also researched this problem online, and I learned that if you leave the faucet open and the water in the pipe thaws, then it could come rushing out and flood the house. I realized that I could not leave the home in this precarious situation. I decided to enlist the help of a kind neighbor, who came over and turned off the water and the water heater for a brief amount of time. My client's backup person arrived soon after. She slowly defrosted the pipes and turned the water heater back on, and the water began running in the left sink once again. When my clients returned from a trip to the Arctic (ironically!), their home was just like they had left it. We were all very thankful that their house was safe, and the water pipes were working well once again. What a relief! I was very grateful to the neighbors and my client's backup person, who saved this house from possible disaster.

DEALING WITH LEAKING PIPES AND PLUMBING AND OIL LEAKS

Similarly, it is always a good idea to check the basement in the client's home. Several times when I was cleaning a litter box in a basement, the cats alerted me to a puddle on the floor. Thinking it might be cat urine, I investigated and found out it was a puddle of water! I thanked the cats in each of these situations for alerting me so I could put a bucket under the drips, contact their pet parents, and save their house from water damage.

In five different houses, I have found that the puddle was from water leaks. Three were leaking water heaters, one was a leak dripping through the ceiling pipe, and another was a leak from a dehumidifier. Fortunately, I found a bucket nearby in each of these houses and put it under the dripping water. I was not sure how much of the bucket would be filled up before my next visit, so I notified my clients or their designated person immediately so they could advise me.

In the case of the leaking water heaters, two of my clients had a heating service company on speed dial to prevent this situation from becoming a catastrophic flood in their basement. The third time I encountered this problem, the clients decided to drive home early and take care of it themselves.

When the leak was dripping from the ceiling pipe, my client asked me to keep a bucket under the leak overnight to see if it got any worse, and to call them the next morning. I put a circular bucket into a larger, rectangle-shaped plastic bin to catch any overflow to be sure no water escaped onto the floor of their basement. Since I was taking care of the kitty twice a day for a week, this approach still seemed safe for their house. I could empty the bucket at each visit and gauge the amount of water that was being collected. However, even though I was the only person in the house, and I was running the same amount of water each day, the amount of dripping water was inconsistent. On one visit, the dripping looked like it was ceasing. Then, on the next visit, the amount of water in the bucket was deeper. Fortunately, my client arrived home to a dry basement. Later, they let me know it was a leak in the toilet just above the basement pipes that had caused this problem.

At another house, I usually entered through the side door, but then I decided that the basement door would be better for their cats' safety. These cats were used to going outside on a leash, and some-times they tried to run out as I entered through the side door. By going in through the basement, which they did not have access to, I eliminated the risk of them escaping. However, as I made this change, I noticed a puddle of water on the basement floor, which I traced to the dehumidifier. Once again there was a bucket nearby, and I was able to place it under the leak to contain the water, so the basement floor did not get any further water damage. Then I contacted their backup person, who came over and fixed the problem with the unit. The wet spot on the floor was dry by the end of my assignment.

Three times, a client's furnace was dripping water. For two of those times, I placed a bucket under the pipe on the furnace, as directed by my client. I emptied the bucket on each of my visits, and they took care of the problem by contacting their service provider.

The third time I noticed this at a client's home, I put a bucket under the drip, thinking it was a slow leak. However, when I returned, the constant drip had flooded the basement. I moved as many items as possible out of the water to a dry area, and then I contacted my client, who gave me a plumber's name and number. I contacted the plumber to set up a repair time, and I agreed to return again later to let the plumber into the house. It is always good to build in some extra time at each assignment for emergencies that may arise, so a time constraint does not create added stress.

I recently encountered yet another challenging situation. As I entered the house for the final kitty-care visit of one of my assignments, I noticed a strong smell of oil! I immediately opened safe windows and investigated the furnace area, but I did not find any oil leakage. I notified my client to see if there had been a recent oil delivery that could explain this smell. My client confirmed that this was possible and asked me to check the oil tank. As I snapped a photo of the filled oil tank, I noticed a spillage of oil on the cement floor. I reported this to my client, who arranged to have the oil delivery company come over to fix the problem after she returned that afternoon. Apparently, as the oil was being pumped into the tank, it had leaked out and spread not only onto the cement floor but also beyond that area onto the main flooring and into another closet. If this had been left unreported to my client and unattended by the oil delivery company, it could have become a very costly problem, plus it would have created an unsafe environment for the kitty.

GETTING LOCKED OUT

How about locking yourself out of the pet's house? Once, I opened the sliding-glass door and went out onto the screened-in porch to take care of the kitty's litter box. Behind me, the stick the clients used for security fell into place along the base of the sliding door—which jammed just enough so that I could not get back into the house. I tried to squeeze through the narrowed opening, but I soon realized I was locked out.

Trying not to panic since the kitties were inside the house looking at me askance, I noticed that although I had no way to get inside to get my keys and cat supply bag, I did have my cellphone in my pocket. I immediately contacted the pet parents, trying to sound calm, and explained that I had locked myself out of their house. They offered a few hopeful ideas, but in the end, I had no way to enter their house.

We decided that I should contact a locksmith to unlock the main door, walk through the house, and open the sliding-glass door so I could get back in. This was an expensive lesson for me to learn about being careful with the security bars on slider doors. Later, when I gave the clients an update, I apologized again for interrupting their vacation, and we discussed payment options for the locksmith because it was my fault and my responsibility.

There was one other time when I was locked out of a house and had to contact the pet parents and then a locksmith. In that situation, the cleaning crew had locked the side door to the garage, but when I arrived, the garage door code did not work. I had no keys to the house, because the clients always used the garage door themselves. This is why I advised earlier to always get a key or fob in hand before you accept a pet sitting job.

Several other times, at two different houses, the garage door code did not work. The keypad battery was dead at one house, and, at the other, the sun was shining at such an angle that it disrupted the garage door system. In each of those cases, I was grateful I had a physical key and the front door entry code so I could get in to care for the kitties; they were hungry and in need of attention and playtime.

DEALING WITH ALARM SYSTEMS

At your initial Meet & Greet, be sure you practice turning any alarms off and on, since there are many different types of alarm systems. Also make sure you know the security password to provide to the alarm company if the alarm goes off, because if the alarm continues to chime and you cannot get it to shut off, the police will show up, and they will have the right to check the premises for safety.

For example, one time I arrived at a home only to discover that an alarm had gone off due to a malfunctioning window sensor. The alarm could not be shut off in the usual way—only through the alarm company. As I was calling the alarm company to give them the security password to deactivate the alarm, police officers arrived and asked to be let in to search the house. Since the alarm served as probable cause, I needed to allow them entry. Fortunately, as soon as the alarm company had the security password, they were able to shut off the alarm remotely.

The police officers thought the cats might have climbed into the sink, where their food bowls were drying, and then onto the windowsill, setting off the alarm. I contacted the client, and they talked with the police officer to be reassured that their home was secure. This was quite a disruptive event for the kitties, our playtime cat games, and the pet parent's vacation!

Another time a smoke detector went off ten feet up in a client's garage—sounding a *Fire! Fire!* alert frequently. The weather was unusually hot, with temperatures in the nineties and one hundreds for many days on end. I was concerned, but I did not detect a fire, and I did not have a ladder to reach and shut off the alarm. To address the situation, I consulted with my client's backup person for house concerns. He thought the extreme heat was causing the smoke detector to go off.

This was not an emergency to us, but to the kitties it was "cat-astrophic"! They were normally very friendly, but now they had disappeared. After I looked and looked for the kitties, I finally noticed two sets of big round eyes looking out at me from beneath a cabinet. They were on high alert, looking stressed and anxious. Poor little kitties. I talked with them and coaxed them out with a fleece string and laser light. The backup person was able to stop by with a ladder and reset the alarm, which, he discovered, had been set off by a bug! The cats and I were very grateful for his assistance and the return of peace and quiet.

NAVIGATING ICE AND SNOW

What if the driveway is not plowed, or it is too icy to travel? I always make sure I am prepared for slippery conditions, and I dress warmly so I can walk up the driveway from the road to the house in cases of deep snow. I always have a shovel in my car, and I joined AAA in case I get stuck in a client's driveway, or if I need a battery or a tow after a breakdown.

I am alert to weather conditions. I leave extra food and water for the pets if I know a storm is coming and I may get delayed. All my clients care about my safety, and they have told me to skip or delay a visit if the roads are too icy or snowy.

Fortunately, only once have I had to notify the pet parents that I could not arrive as scheduled. Extremely icy road conditions were causing my car to slip, slide, and spin around. Because I had been aware of this possibility in advance, I had left extra food for the kitties' evening meal. As I've noted several times throughout the book, all my clients are very understanding of such circumstances, which I really appreciate.

WORKING WITH CLEANERS AND CONTRACTORS

At times I have taken care of pets in the homes of clients who have cleaning crews, although I generally decline these jobs because of potential insurance liabilities. When I do agree, my clients ask me to arrive after the cleaning crew is gone, not at the same time as when they are at the house. This is beneficial to me because I want to check to see if the cats are out of closets and their food, water, and litter are fine. If the cleaning people stress out the kitties while they are using a vacuum and moving around the house, interrupting their sleep and routines, it is best for me not to be associated with these times.

I have had pet sitting jobs when a repair person or contractors have been at the client's house during my visit. This can be extra stressful for kitties, sometimes requiring them to be isolated in a smaller area. Ideally, I know about these workers in advance, but sometimes the clients only mention it after I've started the assignment. In some cases, even the clients were not expecting the person or delivery, such as when a contractor had windows delivered that my client was not expecting. In that case, I immediately notified the client to verify that this contractor was indeed allowed to enter the premises. Then I relocated the kitties—along with their food, water, and litter—to a bedroom that was not part of the construction project, so they were safe during this window installation.

This chapter has covered unexpected challenges directly related to the clients' homes. But as you'll see in the next chapter, sometimes the dilemmas actually concern who—or *what*—is on site when you arrive!

CHAPTER NINE

UNEXPECTED, UNIQUE PETS, OR UNUSUAL EVENTS

Although I seldom decline a pet sitting job, over the years I have come to realize that not everyone, or every situation, falls into a traditional pet sitting "cat-egory." In this chapter, I will share some of the unexpected, unique, or unusual challenges I've faced as I've worked with clients—hopefully, you can learn from these surprises!

SURPRISE GUESTS

One day, I went to take care of a kitty, and although I expected no one to be home, a teenager answered the door. I was startled and asked who she was. She said she was the girlfriend of the boy who lived there. I remained outside of the house and called my clients to verify that she was allowed to be in their home and that it was okay for her to stay there. The clients said she was a good kid, and it was fine with them if she stayed at their house; they also apologized for the surprise, because their son hadn't forewarned them. I went ahead with the kitty-care duties for that day, but I still felt a bit unsettled and uncomfortable.

When I arrived the next day, I found the girlfriend and her friend in the house. They were playing video games in the kitchen area where I usually prepared the cat food and played with the kitty. I had to walk directly past the teenagers to clean the kitty litter. I carefully stepped over wires from the TV screen the girls had pulled out from the wall as I tried not to interrupt the video game that they were intently playing. A brief hello was exchanged.

As this week of pet sitting visits went on, my sense of discomfort increased. I also worried about the condition the house would be left in and the welfare of the kitty; I felt responsible for both.

One day when I arrived, no one seemed to be home, but I was not sure. I needed to know before I set the alarm. As I checked the rooms for the kitty, I noticed the girl was sleeping in an upstairs bedroom. Another awkward moment. I set the alarm with the girl in the house, hoping it would not go off, which could interrupt my clients' vacation and bring emergency services to check on the house. Fortunately, the alarm did not go off.

After I completed the job, I evaluated the personal cost of finding unexpected strangers in the house, worrying if the kitty felt safe or was stressed, knowing my insurance would not cover any issues (since other people were in this house), and having to work around strangers. It was definitely beyond my comfort level, and I decided to decline future jobs from this long-time client. Instead, I referred them to their local veterinarian to seek another pet sitter.

STRANGE VISITORS

Sometimes when I am pet sitting, a stranger comes to the door. Perhaps it is a neighbor, a friend of one of the kids in the family, a campaign worker, or someone selling something.

One time, during campaign season, I answered the front door but left the screen door shut to keep the cats from going outdoors. From the doorstep, the campaign worker asked me lots of questions, like party affiliation and who I was planning to vote for. I did not want them to know I was a pet sitter who did not live in the house, since they could then surmise that my client was away. Instead, I answered the questions in a vague, noncommittal way. This awkward experience helped me to make a policy not to answer the door unless it is clearly an emergency. I also appreciate the doorbell cameras that allow the visitor and my clients to communicate directly with each other.

UNEXPECTED DELIVERIES

What if packages and mail are delivered to your client's house, but they were actually intended for someone else at a different address? It is wise to check all the addresses of letters and packages that arrive, to be sure they actually belong to the client. Once, a long box was left outside my client's house, so I brought the box inside. A few days later, I happened to notice that the label had a different name and address, and I realized that the box probably contained flowers! I quickly dropped off the package at the correct address, with an apology. Similarly, I have dropped off stray letters left for neighbors nearby.

Or what if the package comes to the right name and address, but you're really not sure what to do with it? Another time, eye medication was unexpectedly delivered to my client in dry ice. I couldn't tell what the package contained initially, but it had clear instructions to refrigerate it immediately upon arrival. However, it was too big to fit into the refrigerator.

I was lucky my clients had noticed the delivery through their camera, so when I contacted them, they knew it was eye medication stored in dry ice. They instructed me to use their gloves to take the eye medication out from under the loose dry ice. I was able to leave the dry ice in the container it came in. I learned from Google that dry ice is hazardous to wildlife if it is left outside uncovered. I also learned that dry ice can damage the sink drains and toilet pipes if left to melt in a sink or toilet.

RIGHT PLACE, WRONG TIME

Even when you confirm your assignment one week ahead, there may still be times of miscommunication. What if you go to the house and the clients are actually still there? This has happened to me three times. Once, I opened the front door and the house smelled like bacon—and the sound of a vacuum cleaner let me know that my clients had not left yet. I was startled to realize the people were still home! I scurried out the door and returned later that day.

Another time, in the middle of an assignment, I arrived to find that the clients' mailbox was empty, which was unusual, and their two cars were in the garage. It certainly appeared that they might be home again, so I knocked and was greeted by the husband. I apologized, and we checked our calendars to see what had gone wrong in our communication for my services. In the end my trip was still valuable, because while I was there, the client reviewed the kitty-care process with me again since a few things had changed since our last meeting.

REPLACEMENT SITTERS

Another time, when I went to take care of a kitty, I was surprised that my client's nephew was home from college! In this case, I had not checked my email recently, and the pet parent had sent me a message about this last-minute change. The nephew had decided to come home for a few days, and he had volunteered to take care of the kitty. I apologized to the student and let him know I would be leaving. From this experience, I learned to check my email as well as text messages prior to going to any pet sitting visit.

EXTRA PETS

Over the years, I've learned to check around the house for extra pets. Sometimes the family has forgotten to mention the newly acquired fish or the hamster in a child's bedroom.

It is hard to imagine, but one time I encountered an extra black cat under a bed! I had been hired to take care of one black cat, but this was a second one. Was I seeing double? I quickly took care of both cats and texted the pet parents about this unexpected turn of events. They confirmed there were indeed two black cats. As it turned out, at the last minute, the grandmother had dropped off her black cat for care too, and the client had forgotten to tell me. Expect the unexpected on your pet sitting visits!

UNEXPECTED WILDLIFE

Even after thirty years of experience, I faced a new challenge when a long-time client called me the evening before she was due to leave on her trip to explain that she had a mother raccoon and four babies in her attic! Yikes!

She had contacted a critter control company, and she had a neighbor on the lookout to check her Havahart traps. One trap was under the pine tree the raccoon used to climb up onto the roof to gain access to the ducts and the attic, and the other trap was in the attic. I asked what my responsibility would be in this situation other than protecting the cats from any raccoon interactions and their usual cat care and playtimes. The pet parent asked me to contact her and the neighbor immediately if I saw a raccoon in a trap and then call the critter control company to release the animal as soon as possible. (I later learned that in some cases, if a client's house is part of an association, then the president of the association needs to be involved in situations like this to be sure the rules and bylaws for animal capture and relocation are followed.)

As it turned out, the adventure began with a trapped animal the very next morning! Before the pet parent left, she contacted me to say a skunk was trapped and was being released soon. I thought, *Oh no!* but then I stuck to my responsibility in this adventure, which was providing kitty care, organizing kitty playtimes, and contacting people to assist with the mother and baby raccoons if they were trapped.

On the third day, there was a large sad, wet raccoon trapped under the pine tree during a rainstorm. The raccoon had tipped the Havahart trap on its side. I thought it might be the father and that the whole family could be relocated somewhere else. Come to find out from the critter control company representative I reached on the phone, a father would kill any babies, and this trapped raccoon was probably a different mother than the one using the attic, with her own set of babies somewhere nearby. That was correct! In the attic, the mother raccoon with the four babies were in *that* Havahart trap. Busy day for critter control!

The neighbor agreed to be on call to let the critter control people in later that day, and he was kind enough to bring fresh vegetables to the mother raccoons while he awaited the animals' release. The mother and four babies from the attic were transported to a lake in northern New Hampshire, and the other mother raccoon was released to take care of her babies nearby, which no doubt were anxiously awaiting her return.

A DUCK DOWN THE CHIMNEY

In the very first year I was pet sitting, I got a call from my client who had just arrived home. She asked, "How did everything go?"

I said, "Very well." Then I reiterated some of the cat's adventures, which I had written down on the Pet Care Journal Form and left on their counter.

My client said, "Well, did you notice the duck?"

I was flabbergasted! "The duck!?" I asked. "Wait What!?"

"Yes," she said. "When we came home and opened our front door, a duck came flying out of the house, with the cat chasing the duck closely behind!"

Oh no! It sounded like a cartoon scene. I had no words! I certainly had not noticed anything out of the ordinary, or I would have reported it.

Apparently, the duck had come down one of the three chimneys, which was unscreened. According to my client, the duck hopped up the stairs, ate plants in the breakfast room, and was chased around by the cat. In fact, the poor little duck was attacked by the cat, so there were bloody spots around the living room and on the ceiling. What a mess to clean up—and tough times for the duck being hunted by the cat.

Fortunately, my client was understanding, and she continued to book me for pet sitting for many years to come. And we believe the duck probably lived happily ever after, too!

FISH AND SEAHORSES AND COWS, OH MY!

As a pet sitter, you never know who will contact you and for which type of creature. Be open and curious, educate yourself about each new species, and take good notes at the Meet & Greet. If you agree to take care of exotic fish, goldfish with varying feeding needs, and other creatures, be sure to read up on each species, and ask the pet parent to leave detailed instructions.

Even when you're armed with knowledge, unique pet sitting tasks can get challenging. One cold winter night, the electricity went off in a client's house, where I was taking care of two cats and the family's exotic fish. They did not have a generator, and without electricity, the heater was off in the tank. Quickly thinking outside the box, I decided to wrap blankets around the large tank to help retain the heat. These fish survived, but I was very worried.

Once when I was in a house, I noticed the temperature was dropping to around 58°F. I contacted the pet parents, who confirmed that the thermostat was intentionally set to a low temperature. I continued to be worried about the goldfish and debated whether to take it to my house. I decided against it, because it seemed risky to take the fish in its bowl out in freezing temperatures and then get it used to new surroundings. On my last visit, the fish was eating and swimming around and seemed fine with the temperature, so I thought all was well.

Sadly, my clients later told me that the fish passed away a few days after my last visit, and I felt terrible. Apparently, the red switch on the wall connected to the furnace had been inadvertently switched off by my client, so the temperature eventually dropped even lower than they had anticipated. Now that I've had that experience, if I notice the thermostat getting lower than expected in a client's home, I first check the red wall switch to be sure the heater is on.

On a happier note, on one assignment I successfully cared for two female seahorses that lived in a saltwater tank. Since seahorses do not have teeth or even a stomach, their digestive process functions with extraordinary rapidity. I had to squirt tiny shrimp into their mouth! I loved watching them eat and float elegantly around.

When I did some research, I learned that seahorses have sharp eyesight and can see forward and backward simultaneously. Further, they can hear low humming noises, and they make clicking sounds to communicate with each other.

According to their pet parent, these seahorses were wild-caught versus farm raised. They engaged in a unique courtship dance when one was ready to lay eggs. They were both female; therefore, one of them laid eggs on the bottom of the saltwater tank. Typically, the female will transfer the eggs into the male's pouch, and the male will fertilize and incubate the 100's of eggs, until they are fully developed, around 24 days. Then the male will spew the baby seahorses out of his pouch. Larger seahorses live to around 4 years of age. Based on the frequent feedings per day because seahorses do not have stomachs and the maintenance of a salt water tank, I was advised by this pet parent not to have seahorses as pets.

The seahorses needed specialized care, with frequent feedings and cleaning of their saltwater tank, and the pet parent eventually decided to donate them to a local science center, where they enjoyed a huge tank. What an extraordinary experience taking care of and watching these unique and elegant sea creatures!

I also had the pleasure of taking care of two Belted Galloway cows and their two calves, which were adorable. Initially, I was a bit afraid of the mother cows, thinking they would be protective of their young. For the cow family's safety, I decided to climb through the fence slats because I was not about to open the gate and be stampeded or let this cow family loose. Even so, the cows, calves, and I got along very well. I was able to walk around their pasture, add water to their heated metal trough, and give them yogurt treats left by their pet parents.

As you have seen throughout these chapters, there is much to consider when you are responsible for people's animal companions, plants, and homes. Be prepared to continue learning and problem solving throughout your career—even after many years of experience!

CHAPTER TEN

CAT ENRICHMENT GAMES AND ACTIVITIES

As I've stressed throughout this book, I always make time to play with the cats. My goal is to provide engagement for the kitties using interactive games to "cat-ch" their attention, heighten their interest, and ensure that they have a fun time with me—and vice versa. There is scientific evidence that patting and relaxing with animals also lowers people's blood pressure.

Many of the cats I care for enjoy cat enrichment activities after they have eaten (or sometimes when I first arrive at their home). As I mentioned in the section on aging kitties, I have found that even very senior cats enjoy enrichment activities such as tracking the laser light and watching fleece string toys that act like snakes. I always try to make their toys come alive with mouse-like behaviors.

When I plan games and activities for each cat sitting assignment, I try to provide a multisensory experience for each kitty based on what they like to do. I create games to stimulate their visual and hearing skills, eye-paw coordination, and sense of smell and touch—with lots of pats and purrs in between to help them feel safe and secure. They all have different likes and dislikes, and they make their preferences known. On the Pet Care Journal Form, I describe the kitty's adventures and highlight their favorite cat games.

The best part of the cat enrichment games is that we have such a great time together. In this chapter, I will provide more details about how these games and activities work. The Resources section also includes links to help you find similar options. At the end of this chapter, I also discuss brushing—an activity some cats really enjoy.

STALKING GAMES

Most cats enjoy stalking, chasing, and pouncing on their toys when I throw the toys into the air. Based on the fact that the cats often move the toys between my visits, I know that some kitties also like to play with their toys on their own.

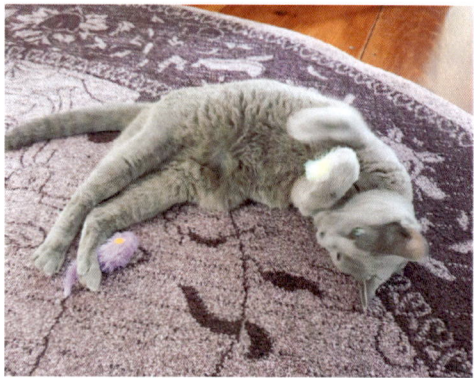

Some cats enjoy toy and ball games that we play on the staircase. The kitty perches on the stair and remains on high alert as I toss a ball or a toy into the air. Many cats enjoy catching the toys, and some even bat the ball back to me.

LASER LIGHT GAMES

One of their most loved visual games is chasing the laser light. There are certain houses I would not dare show up at now without the laser light—the kitties would be very disappointed. I advise purchasing a laser light that stays on and has a flashlight option, which will help you find hiding cats.

I am careful never to get the laser light in the kitty's eye. I also allow for rest time, which I can gauge by looking at the kitty's breathing rate. Some kitties get very obsessed and play until they are exhausted. Kittens are especially vulnerable to this obsession, and they need breaks to recover and breathe normally.

If you don't have a laser light yet, or if you have forgotten it, you can often use jewelry instead. If you allow the sun to shine on your watch, or maybe a ring, you may be able to create a reflection of light on the wall to amuse the cat, just like the laser light.

ONLINE CAT GAMES

Online cat games are also available to improve visual skills and eye-paw coordination. Many are even free!

Mouse in Cheese and Mouse for Cats

Another favorite cat game is Mouse in Cheese, which I let the cats play on my tablet. In this game, the cats watch mice as they glide out of a block of cheese across the screen. The cats learn that when they pounce, the mouse squeaks and disappears under their paw. Some kitties use one paw, some use two paws, and some even use their nose!

Another popular online cat game is Mouse for Cats. The mouse changes colors after the cat pounces on it many times. The mouse even looks like it is breathing, because its chest goes in and out.

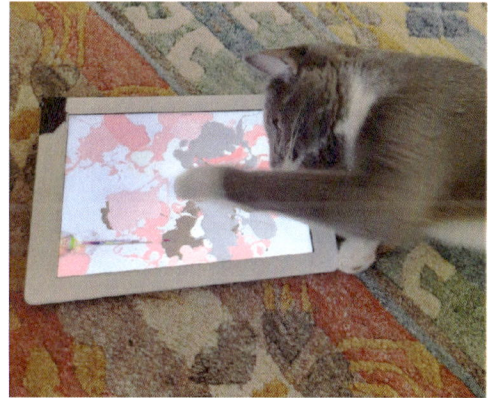

Many cats think the mouse has gone under the tablet when it exits through the side of the screen, and they are very engaged.

Magic Fluids Lite, Fluid Simulation, and Acrylic Paint Project

There are several other favorite online cat games, such as Magic Fluids Lite and Fluid Simulation on Google Play, and Acrylic Paint Project on Apple.

Using these apps, I can give the kitties painting lessons. Magic Fluids, which has music in the background, lets the kitties create and watch colorful fluid patterns. This seems to mesmerize them! Using my finger to teach them how to play, I encourage the kitties to use their paw to pounce on swirling designs on the screen. As the cat pounces on the swirls, colored designs appear, then disappear. With Acrylic Paint Project, you can teach the cats how to tap the screen and help them change the colors as they pounce on the screen to create paint dots. With Fluid Simulation, after you teach the cat to tap the screen, they can make colorful swirls.

As they paw the tablet, they make lovely paintings. The cats look forward to the art classes during my visit, and I save their designs by taking a photo or screenshot. Later, I can send this photo to the pet parent by text or email, or I can print this masterpiece as a gift for a holiday or birthday surprise.

Creature Simulators

With the Dmitsoft apps, the cats can enjoy Mouse simulator, a game that allows the cat to pounce on mice. Cat Game - Game for Cats! Marsel Gilyazov, the cat can pounce on a mouse, cheese, bird, fish, butterfly, fly and bee as they travel across the screen.

Cat Fishing

With the Cat Fishing 2 app by Nestle Purina Petcare/Friskies, the kitties can watch and pounce on fish swimming across the screen. When their paw touches the screen, the fish wiggles away, and the water makes a splashing sound. If I am taking care of an anxious kitty, I find this app engages their hunting instincts, which helps to calm them.

HIDE AND SEEK

Hide and Seek for some kitties is lots of fun. I hide behind a sofa or in another room altogether. Some kitties locate me immediately and get lots of praise and pats. Other kitties get scared because I look like a predator to them as I am crawling on the floor, hiding, and peeking out at them, so I switch to another game they like better.

MUSIC AND BIRD SOUNDS

To calm (or stimulate) the cats' auditory senses, I play relaxing cat music from the app RelaxMyCat by Relax My Dog Ltd and relaxing wild bird sounds on YouTube. Some cats go on high alert when they hear the bird sounds. They race around their house and then locate the sounds coming from my phone. I watch their reactions to see if this game is fun or frustrating for them. Some cats enjoy looking our the window for wildlife watching squirrels, turkeys, chipmunks and birds.

NAME RESPONSE

It's easy to play games with the cats even without the use of technology. For this simple game, I call their names to see if they respond in some way. Most cats do recognize and respond to their names.

CATNIP TOYS

As noted, I don't bring my own catnip toys to homes. However, many clients' homes already have these catnip toys, and they give me permission to use them. In those cases, to perk up the kitties' olfactory senses, I refreshen the catnip toys by squeezing them to activate the catnip smell.

CATNIP BUBBLES

Catnip bubbles are usually made of water, unscented castile soap (which is safe for cats), catnip (fresh or dried), and optional corn syrup to make them last longer. You can purchase these online, buy them at your local pet store, or make the bubbles yourself after confirming with the clients that the cats are fine with catnip. Initially, the kitty will look at these whimsical bubbles and be mystified or a bit nervous. After they become more familiar with the game, many cats enjoy sniffing, pouncing on, and catching the bubbles in midair. Cats are so talented!

Some cats do not—and never will—like bubble play. These cats growl at them. One of my clients has three cats. One cat loves the bubbles, one growls at the bubbles, and one ignores the bubbles. However, all of the cats seem to enjoy sniffing where the bubbles have landed and rolling around in this catnip scent. It is a challenge getting a photo of the kitty leaping and pawing to catch a bubble, but when I can, my clients love it!

MOTORIZED TOYS

For multisensory experiences, many cats enjoy interactive, motorized toys that simulate the catching of prey. For instance, some cats enjoy a motorized ball with a built-in tail that rolls around the room in different directions. A lot of these toys are rechargeable, and many will go into sleep mode after a while to save the charge. Some of these toys even chirp or make other sounds. They also make birds with wings that flap—and even fish! Some of these toys have removable shells that are washable, too.

FLEECE STRINGS

Sometimes, simplicity is the most popular choice. The favorite toy of many cats I care for is a rainbow-colored fleece string attached to the end of a plastic stick. This toy is very flexible, safe, durable, and easy to clean.

This game has many options. When I pull the rainbow-colored fleece string behind me, the kitties naturally stalk and pounce on it.

145

When I wave it in the air, the cats leap for it. Sometimes I also move the stick around so they think it's a living creature. I hide it under rugs and newspapers—with the string poking out just enough so it looks like prey. The kitty can stalk it and then pounce on it.

I buy a fleece string for each household and wash it in between visits with unscented castile soap, a cat-safe soap. The kitties who have climbing posts enjoy stalking and chasing their fleece strings up onto the posts or inside their tunnels. They stalk, leap, and pounce for exercise and fun!

STUFFED TOYS

Many cats love to catch their toys midair with one or two snatches. It is so cute watching the kitty sitting straight up and then leaping in the air to catch their favorite stuffed toys. This activity also makes great photos for their pet parents to enjoy. As I play with the cats, I compliment each of them on their amazing acrobatic talents.

THE TREAT GAME

During my visits, some kitties look at me to hand them a treat, but I prefer to encourage their hunting instincts by hiding the treats (or kibble) and asking them to find it. To start, I show the kitties the first treat so they know where it is hiding. Then I watch as their eyes become large, their body goes on alert, and their nose starts to sniff as they hunt to find the other delicious treats around their home.

Some kitties catch on quickly and remind me if I forget about the Treat Game. Other cats are not that interested, and they train me to bring them a treat.

LOUNGING

Not all cats enjoy lively activities, and even those that do sometimes simply love to lounge. During these quieter periods, I sit nearby and talk to them. I play relaxing music, and I show them creatures playing online through the apps I've already mentioned.

Cats are well-known loungers. Most kitties enjoy relaxing after eating and playing, and I'm happy to take this break with them.

BRUSHING

As you've seen, at the Meet & Greet I ask the pet parent if their cat likes to be brushed. If so, I use a cat brush the pet parent leaves out for me. Brushing the cat is a good way to bond with the kitty and help to prevent mats. Be sure to watch the kitty's behavior to know when they have had enough so you do not get swatted at and scratched.

FINAL THOUGHTS

I love all my furry cat friends—as well as the cows, seahorses, and fish I have cared for—and I am entertained by their antics on a daily basis. I have gotten quite attached to the plants, as well, and I take their needs very seriously. All the pet parents love their animal companions as they would a child, and I appreciate the opportunity to care for the animals while my clients are away.

As a bonus, in addition to my salary and the personal satisfaction of helping my clients out, I have so many fun memories of amusing cat antics and amazing photos of their adorableness. Each furry friend has his or her own specific personality, likes, dislikes, needs, and wants that they "train" me to provide for them. I am amazed that they can communicate so well without using any words! They share so much love and affection; it is a pleasure being in their presence.

Here are some final photos of the memorable antics I've encountered during my cat sitting visits.

Throughout this book, I've shared all the tools and qualities that successful pet sitters need:

- Time and flexibility
- A sufficient budget
- Reliable transportation
- Attention to detail on the job and with recordingkeeping
- The ability to follow all the pet parent's instructions
- Excellent communication skills with clients and veterinary staff
- An interest in furthering your knowledge about animal and plant care
- Love and patience with all your clients (human and animal)

If you believe you are a great fit for this amazing profession, then I truly hope you will take the next steps to set up your own pet sitting business. Even after thirty years, I feel this job is extremely rewarding—and I hope you will too! I wish you good luck in all your endeavors as you realize the joy of a pet sitting career and make your dreams come true.

APPENDIX A:

SAMPLE BUDGET

Note: These costs were accurate at the beginning of 2025, but your actual costs may vary. Also note that some of the startup fees, like setting up a website, will turn into related ongoing fees you will need to factor into your budget moving forward, such as maintaining the website, restocking your business cards, and so forth.

ITEM	TYPICAL COST	STARTUP, ONGOING, OR OPTIONAL
Supplies		
Scooper (metal)	$9.00	Startup
Dustpan and brush	$11.00	Startup
Biodegradable or compostable cat litter bags (300 count)	$44.00	Ongoing; costs will depend on the number of clients you have
Scissors	$12.00	Startup
Plant Water Meter (Dr.meter)	$10.00	Startup

154

ITEM	TYPICAL COST	STARTUP, ONGOING, OR OPTIONAL
Castile safe cat soap (16 oz.)	$12.00	Ongoing
Baggies (9 x 12 in., 100-count, biodegradable), for forms	$22.00	Ongoing
Cat Toys		
Rechargeable laser light	$10.00	Startup
Catnip bubbles (2-pack)	$14.00	Ongoing
Fleece string	$9.99	Startup
Marketing & Communication		
Pet Care Journal Forms, Pet Sitting Information Forms, Veterinary Release Forms	$ .55/page	Ongoing
Business cards (100 copies)	$30.00	Ongoing
Flyers (100 copies)	$55.00	Ongoing
Initial Website Design including Domain/Hosting/SLL/Site Lock	$100.00 – $1000.00	Ongoing
Holiday gifts and postage	$300.00	Optional
Advertising	$100.00	Ongoing
Cellphone and internet plans	$2000.00	Ongoing
Business Registration, Fees, and Expenses		
Limited Liability Company fees	$100.00	Startup
State Annual Report Fee	$102.00 (annual)	Ongoing
Trademark name	$50.00 (every 5 years)	Ongoing

ITEM	TYPICAL COST	STARTUP, ONGOING, OR OPTIONAL
Business Liability Insurance as a Sole Proprietor Pet Sitter through (PSI)	$295.00 (annual)	Ongoing
Membership fee Pet Sitters International	$155.00 (annual)	Ongoing
Pet First Aid Class – Red Cross	$25.00	Ongoing
Tax Preparer	$275.00 (annual)	Ongoing
State, Federal, and FICA taxes	Varies by state and your income	Ongoing
PayPal & Venmo fees	1.9% – 3.5% of the transaction	Ongoing
Background check	$25.00 (annual)	Ongoing
Transportation		
Car Insurance	$644.00 (annual)	Ongoing
AAA Roadside Assistance	$64.00 (annual)	Ongoing
Car financing (example is for a lease for the 2025 Honda CR-V, based on TrueCar.com)	$2000 due at signing; $382 per month for a 36-month term, 12,000 miles per year	Ongoing (unless your car is paid off)
Maintenance Fund (e.g., oil changes, tire rotation)	$30 – $100 +	Ongoing
Repair Fund (recommended); will depend on age of car, condition, etc.	$1200 (annual)	Ongoing

ITEM	TYPICAL COST	STARTUP, ONGOING, OR OPTIONAL
Fuel	Driving 12,000 miles with 30 MPG = 400 gallons of gas. With a gas price of $3.75 / gallon, your total cost will be: $1,500 (annually)	Ongoing
Registration	$475.00 (annually - varies by car and state)	Ongoing
Inspection	$45.00 (varies by state)	Ongoing

APPENDIX B:

PET SITTING INFORMATION FORM

PET SITTING INFORMATION

Person's Name: Address:

Cell phone Number: Email:

Pet's Name:

Age: Sex: Breed:

Dates of Pet Care:

Diet:

Veterinarian's Name: Phone Address:

Phone Number:

Medical Information: Any Vomiting, stool concerns, sensitivity to certain foods, catnip, treats:

Mail taken in: Plant care: Light on/off:

Alarm System Instructions: Garage door Code:

Litter Instructions:

Try out Key: Who else has a key?
Your backup person's name_____ Cell phone number

House Care: Heat set at _____AC set at _____ Water shutoff_____

Please text me at _____when you arrive home so I know you are home safe with your kitties.

Payment: Fee is _____/ visit. Will you pay now, leave cash or a check or use PayPal or Venmo?

APPENDIX C:

SAMPLE CAT SITTING CONTRACT

Note: This sample Cat Sitting Contract should not be construed as legal advice and is for informational use only. The enforceability of contracts can vary significantly based on local laws and individual situations. It is strongly recommended that you consult with an attorney in your jurisdiction to ensure that any legal document meets the specific requirements of your area and addresses the unique needs of your business. By using any part of this sample, you acknowledge there is no liability on the part of this author.

CAT SITTING CONTRACT

The Cat Sitting Contract (the "Contract") is entered into on _____

("the effective date") between _____ The Cat Sitter

Company name _____

Company Address _____

Phone Number _____

Client name _____

Address _____

Phone Number _____

Services:

The Cat Sitter shall care for the client's cats as described herein:

Start Date: _____ End Date: _____

Number of visits per day _____ Fee per visit _____

30 minutes _____ 45 minutes _____ 60 minutes _____ Overnight stays _____

CAT INFORMATION:

Name: _____ Age: _____

Gender: _____ Breed: _____

Food and water instructions: _____

_____

Medication instructions: _____

_____

Instructions for Special Needs: _____

_____

Plant care Indoors _____ Outdoors (additional fee) _____

Responsibilities of Cat Sitter. The Cat Sitter shall:

- ☐ Provide food and clean water and necessary medications as directed.
- ☐ Clean the litter daily.
- ☐ Spend quality time playing games with the kitty.
- ☐ Keep the client informed about the cat's well-being.
- ☐ Notify the Client of any unusual events that occur at their home.
- ☐ Other: _____

Payments

PAYMENT METHOD:

Check _____ Cash _____ Payment at the Meet & Greet or left at 1st visit _____

Electronic Payments: Venmo/PayPal prepaid _____
Paid after visit _____

Credit Card: Type of card
Visa _____ M/C _____ Amex _____ Discover _____ Debit _____

Name as it appears on the card _____
Card Number _____ Expiration date _____
Security Code _____

Payment after return from trip _____

Cancellation Policy: If the client cancels _____ days before the start date, a full refund will be provided. If the Client cancels _____ days before the start day, a _____% cancellation fee will be charged.

Emergency Policy

In case of a medical emergency, the Cat Sitter will attempt to contact the Client immediately. If the Client cannot be reached, the Cat Sitter is authorized by the signed Veterinary Release form to seek veterinary care for the cat. The Client is responsible for all veterinary expenses.

The Cat Sitter will do their best to come during inclement weather emergencies but if unable to will leave extra food and water. The Client will have a backup person to attend to the cat if the Cat Sitter is unable to take care of the cat during an emergency. The Cat Sitter cannot be held responsible to any damage to the home or injury to the cat arising from such.

If there is a problem with pipe rupture, flooding, earthquake, fire, or break in, the Cat Sitter will make every effort to reach the client and will follow their instructions. If the Client is unreachable or immediate action is necessary for the health, safety, and welfare of the cat, the Client authorizes the Cat Sitter to make all repairs necessary by the Cat Sitter. The Client agrees to reimburse the Cat Sitter for all expenses for the repairs and will hold the Cat Sitter not responsible for work completed by third parties.

Termination

The Contract shall be terminated automatically on _____. The key will be returned as requested. This contract may be terminated by either Party at any time for no reason by notification either verbal or written.

Liability

The utmost of care will be given in taking care of your cats while in your home. However, due to unpredictability of animals, the Cat Sitter cannot accept responsibility for any mishaps of an extraordinary nature, such as injury, loss, or death of the cat that occurs during the term of this Contract.

Key/Access

The Client agrees to provide the necessary keys and/or alarm and access codes and a clear pathway to the safest door to enter the premises. The Client will make the Cat Sitter aware of their use of cameras and police house checks for security purposes. In case a locksmith is required to gain entry to the Client's premises due to a malfunction of the lock, it shall be the Client's responsibility to reimburse for all costs incurred. The Cat Sitter will try to reach the Client but if unsuccessful, the Client gives the Cat Sitter authority to employ a locksmith on the Client's behalf to gain entry to the house. The Client will notify the Cat Sitter if anyone else has a key or access to the premises. The Cat Sitter will not be held liable for any damage done to the home or cat by a third party. The Cat Sitter shall not be liable for any claim made by any third party.

Governing Law

This Contract shall be governed by laws of the State of _____.

Entire Agreement

By signing below, the Parties acknowledge that they have read, understood, and agree to the terms and conditions submitted in this Cat Sitting Contract.

Cat Sitter's Signature _____

Date _____

Client's Signature _____

Date _____

APPENDIX D:

VETERINARY RELEASE FORM

VETERINARY RELEASE FORM

Owner's Full Name _____

Address _____

Phone Number _____

TO WHOM IT MAY CONCERN:

I hereby authorize the attending Veterinarian or designated Veterinarian _____

to treat my pet(s) in a medical emergency and I accept full responsibility for all fees and charges incurred in the treatment of any of my pet(s).

Name: _____ Age _____ Sex _____ Breed _____

Name: _____ Age _____ Sex _____ Breed _____

Name: _____ Age _____ Sex _____ Breed _____

Name: _____ Age _____ Sex _____ Breed _____

Name: _____ Age _____ Sex _____ Breed _____

The Pet Sitter is authorized to transport my pet(s) to and from the Veterinary Clinic for treatment or to request "onsite" treatment if deemed necessary. If I cannot be reached in case of emergency, the Pet Sitter shall act on my behalf to authorize any treatment.

Tried to contact my Client: _____ Date _____ Time _____

Able to reach Client: YES _____ NO _____

Pet Sitter Signature _____

Owners/Client's Signature _____

Date _____

RESOURCES AND SUGGESTED READINGS

WEBSITES

Whenever I encounter a problem, I look for possible solutions online. Here are some terrific websites that are chock-full of information and educational opportunities.

Pet Sitting Associations and Forums

- *www.petsit.com*: Pet Sitters International provides information on certification, courses, contracts, and forms, plus their "find a pet sitter" database

- *Facebook – Professional Pet Sitters CHAT*: You can request to join this group, run by Pet Sitters International, which provides updates on pet sitters' concerns, help with ideas from other professionals, and current trends

- *www.petsitters.org*: The website of the National Association of Professional Pet Sitters, which offers certification, a locator, conferences, and other services

Plant Care Websites and Apps

- *www.drmeter.com* or Amazon: Tools to test the moisture levels of soil

- *Botan:* Plant Identifier App: AI-generated app identifies plants and offers advice for care

- *Plant Parent: Plant Care Guide App:* Promises to help you "become an instant green thumb and keep your plants not just happy, but thriving!"

Cat Care and Education Websites

- *www.aspca.org/pet-care/animal-poison-control/cats-plant-list*: List of toxic and nontoxic plants

- *www.aspca.org/pet-care/cat-care*: Enrichment games, general cat care, grooming and nutrition tips, common diseases, and behavior issues

- *www.catster.com:* Facts about cat behavior and medical concerns

- *Healthy Cats at www.webmd.com:* Cat symptoms and what they may signify

- *www.redcross.org/take-a-class/classes/cat-and-dog-first-aid-online/a6R0V0000015EUf.html*: "35-minute online course covers understanding your pet's vital signs, breathing and cardiac emergencies, wounds and bleeding, seizures, and preventative care" (current price is $25)

- *www.tufts.catnip.com*: Subscribe to *Catnip Newsletter* to learn about cat medical concerns and behaviors

- *www.vet.cornell.edu/departments-centers-and-institutes/ cornell-feline-health-center/health-information/feline-health-topics/feline-behavior-problems-aggression*: A useful list of behavioral issues and causes

Business Support

- *www.capterra.com/pet sitting-software*: Compares more than thirty products to help you determine what might work best for your business

- *www.forbes.com/advisor/business/paypal-vs-venmo*: A good comparison of payment options

- *www.irs.gov*: Information about business expenses and taxes

- *www.networksolutions.com*: Website hosting and design tools for small businesses

- *www.sba.gov/business-guide/plan-your-business/write-your-business-plan*: Support to help you create a business plan, along with downloadable examples

- *www.wix.com*: Templates and AI tools to help you build a website

- *www.wix.com/tools/business-name-generator*: Free business name generator

Marketing Websites

- *www.canva.com*: A design site with many options to help you "create professional designs and to share or print them"

- *www.care.com*: A website that allows you to list your services and helps people find childcare, senior care, special needs care, pet care, housekeeping, and tutors

- *www.design.com*: Options for designing logos, business cards, social media pages, etc.

- *logosportswear.com*: Offering custom apparel and promotional products

- *www.nextdoor.com*: Offers an app for local neighborhoods that lets people share tips, items for sale, and references for services.

- *www.vistaprint.com*: An affordable source for business cards, banners, personalized gifts, and other promotional items

Sources for Toys, Apps, and Games

It's always a great idea to support your local pet stores and craft fairs. Other sources for toys include online stores like Amazon and Chewy, Apple App Store, or Android Play Store. As noted, some of my cat clients' favorite games are Mouse in Cheese by Petr Vanek; Mouse for Cats by PetrV-koz-IT; Mouse simulator by Dmitsoft; Magic Fluids Lite by Mad Scientist; Cat Fishing 2 by Nestle Purina Petcare; Fluid Simulation by DoGreat Technologies; Acrylic Paint Project by Dando on Line ltd; Fluid Sim by Standard Magic LLC; and Cat Game - Game for Cats! Marsel Gilyazov.

BOOKS AND MAGAZINES

Delgado, Mikel Marie PhD. 2024. *Play with Your Cat: The Essential Guide to Interactive Play for a Happier, Healthier Feline.* New York: TarcherPerigee.

Evans, Jenn. 2024. *Cat Lover's Guide to Feline Health & Wellness.* Independently Published.

Inside Your Cat's Mind: What They Really Think. Single issue magazine. Published by a360 Media

Jeffrey, C. 2022. *Repairing the Heartbreak of Pet Loss.* Independently Published.

Mau, Jia. 2024. *The Ultimate Guide to Understanding Your Cat.* Independently Published.

Pitcairn, Richard H., D.V.M, Ph.D. 2017. *Dr. Pitcairn's Complete Guide to Natural Health for Dogs & Cats.* Emmaus, PA: Rodale Press.

ACKNOWLEDGMENTS

I am very grateful for assistance from my brother, who was not only the first reader and editor of my book but also the researcher and creative designer of my flyers and an ongoing supporter of all my endeavors. My wonderful friend and fellow author, Susan Craig, has been a reader, an idea generator, and a continual cheerleader. Renee Nicholls, my developmental editor, provided expertise, enthusiasm, and "pawsitivity" to bring this book to its successful completion. I wish to thank Sarah Lahay, the fabulous designer of the cover, all the interior and back cover. Sarah is outstanding to work with and incredibly creative as you can see from the uniquely colored edges and easily referenced color-coded chapters and photo placements. Her organization and design expertise made this book come to life. My niece, Katrin Schumann, who is also an author, helped me with layout ideas and provided outstanding writing support. Their inspiring conversations and brilliant insights were invaluable in the development and completion of this book.

I wish to thank my amazing, inspiring husband, Christopher, who introduced me to the love of cats through our first cat, Secret. Christopher has given me years of love and support, and he has helped me thrive in my professional life as a licensed mental health counselor, as a professional pet sitter, as an animal communicator, and now as an author.

I would like to thank my longtime friends Janet Moore, Em Rand, Rose Ciesla, and Kendra and Roy Nagy, who patiently listened to my endless thoughts about this book and assisted with the final cover design choice. I would like to thank a fellow author and Pet Sitter, Amy Kelley for her insights into publishing and marketing. Amy connected me other authors and related events in our community.

I wish to thank Mary Marcinkowski, who helped me find my editor, Renee Nicholls, and connected me with the Newburyport Literary Festival.

I am very grateful to my amazing sister-in-law, who, along with my brother, offered design and content ideas from the very beginning of this venture.

I wish to thank all the staff at the New Hampshire SPCA, specifically Paula Parisi, Humane Education Director. Paula was an excellent Director and teacher of animal care practices that were responsible, educational and fun for all. I greatly appreciate the endorsement from Lisa Dennison, President & CEO, who taught me about legislative issues and increased my understanding of animal welfare issues. I'd also like to thank The International Association of Professional Pet Sitters for their commitment to educating professional pet sitters. Further, I am grateful for the veterinary techs at the North Hampton Animal Hospital, as well as Dr. John Means, Dr. Craig Kelleher, and Dr. Kristen Maloney, who were a reliable referral resource for Pets & Petals, as well as our trusted veterinarians. Similar thanks must also go to the veterinary techs at the Health and Wellness Animal Hospital, and to Dr. Shawna Chag and Dr. Emily Casey, for their expertise in acupuncture, nutritional counseling, and medical care for our pets. The knowledge I have gained from these professionals—along with the reassurance of always knowing they are there for backup in medical emergencies—has enhanced my pet sitting business.

I also wish to thank all the amazing animals in my care throughout the years that have taught me so much about individuality, preferences, viewpoints, and love. I appreciate that they've shared their loving feelings and homes with me. I also must thank the cats who have shared my own home, because their love has taught me so much: Sookie and Wink (currently) and, over the past years, Secret, Misty, Kali, Pumpkin, Patsy, Whisper, and Silky. These kitties were all adopted from the New Hampshire SPCA, except for Patsy, who joined us from the home of my Grandmother Lu Lu Dougherty when she passed away at 106 years of age. Our cats are such loving beings, and I will honor and cherish them always.

ABOUT THE AUTHOR

Diane O'Callahan lives with her husband, Christopher, and their cats: Sookie, a white long-haired Manx, and Wink, a buff and white Turkish Van. In the photo to the left, Diane is holding Silky and standing near Whisper, two cats that are currently living in Heaven.

These sweet kitties are adoptees from the New Hampshire SPCA, and they have helped her become a better pet sitter.

Diane can be reached through
www.petsandpetals.us.